HISTORY OF
THE SHINE FAMILY IN
EUROPE AND AMERICA

BY
JOHN W. SHINE

Published by Left of Brain Books

Copyright © 2021 Left of Brain Books

ISBN 978-1-396-32207-5

First Edition

Table of Contents

PREFACE.

In attempting to write the history of a family one meets with many difficulties. The most reliable information to be obtained for a work of this kind is, of course, the records. But it is an endless undertaking to search for records, hidden by years of time, and scattered far and wide. And as such a history begins at a time when few records were kept, and but few of them preserved, the difficulty in procuring satisfactory data is quite apparent. After tracing back only a few generations it becomes very uncertain, and unsatisfactory.

In obtaining data from those who know, or should know, something of their immediate family history, you are also met with difficulties. Very few take interest enough in their family history to take the time to furnish information to make a satisfactory and complete history of the family.

At first my object was simply to track back my own immediate family to its origin, but in doing so I gathered much information of other families of the name, and concluded to put it all in book form, that it may aid others in writing a more accurate and complete history of the family Shine, or in locating relatives.

I desire to acknowledge my indebtedness to:

Rev. P. Wolfe, of Kilmallock, Ireland; Rev. P. Ring, of Ballyclough, Ire.; Junius Augustus Shine, of Faison, N. C.; David Shepard Shine, of Jacksonville, Fla.; Walter R. Bozeman, of Atlanta, Ga; Francis Eppes Shine, M. D., of Bisbee, Arizona; Patrick C. Shine, of Spokane, Wash.; Daniel Shine Jones, of New Bern, N. C.; Eugene Shine, of Downeyville, Ont.; George Shine, of Lindsay, Ont.; Miss Julia Shine, of Cleveland, Ohio, and Mrs. Alice Banks, of Indianapolis Ind., for their valuable assistance in furnishing data and material for this work. I am also very thankful to many others who kindly answered my letters.

John W. Shine.

Sault Ste. Marie, Mich.,
    May 1st, 1917.

JOHN W. SHINE.

THE FAMILY OF "SHINE" IN IRELAND, ENGLAND AND SCOTLAND.

CHAPTER I.

From the remotest time, man has endeavored to preserve his genealogy and family ancestry. Long before the recording of events was practiced it was not unusual to find persons who could, from memory, trace their lineage far back through a long line of ancestors into the remote ages.

In Homer's time men were inspired to noble and heroic deeds by recounting to them the valor and prowess of their ancestors for three and four generations back. And the people of nearly every country have, in some way or another, kept records of family genealogy. There were many reasons for doing so. It was a natural instinct to know of parents, grandparents and great grandparents through their memory being conveyed from father to son, and through family traditions. It was also important in the descent of property and other heraldic rights to keep a correct account of the line of ancestry.

After writing came in use records were more easily kept and preserved. And in more recent years printing made it still more easily to record and preserve family genealogies. Unfortunately, however, most of the countries have, in time, been devastated by war, and overrun by tribes and people who did not appreciate the preservation of records, or realize their value, so that much of the records in most every country have been lost or destroyed, making it quite difficult in many cases to trace back, with any degree of satisfaction, the genealogy of any family for many centuries.

The changes in the spelling of names also adds to the difficulties in tracing the names back from one generation to another. Then again as surnames only came in general use in the eleventh century, when we attempt to trace back beyond that period, we find the task a most difficult one, and if it were not for the fact that a few scattering records have come down through all the wreck and ruin of ages to guide us in our research, all would have been lost in the buried centuries of the past. But with such records as have survived, we can, by comparison and analyzation, trace out, with a certain degree of accuracy, the genealogy of most families for many centuries back. To trace the genealogy of any family one will be impressed with the devious winding course, the intermixing of family trees and crossing and recrossing of ancestral lines, and the great number of different family lines that are connected. It shows, as suggested by Hart:

"How every race and every creed
    Might be by love combined;
Might be combined, yet not forget
    The fountains whence they rose,
As filled by many a rivulet
    The stately Shannon flows."

CHAPTER II.

ORIGIN OF THE FAMILY NAME "SHINE."

The name "Shine" is found in Ireland, England and Scotland, but principally in Ireland. It is rarely found in any of the other countries of Europe, Asia or Africa, especially for any distance back. We must look, therefore, to Ireland, England and Scotland for the origin of the name, or the earliest record of the name as a family name.

It is claimed by some, and particularly by one well known author and genealogist, that the name Shine is an English name of Saxon origin. Mr. Josiah H. Shinn, in his "History of the Shinn Family," gives considerable space to the origin of the name Shinn. He shows that the name Shinn is derived from the name Shine and endeavors to establish the Saxon origin of the name. He concludes that the name is derived from the Saxon root word "Sinn," which finds its counterpart in the Suevian "Senn." He thinks the intrusion of the "h" in Sinn may have been for euphony; if not, then, to destroy the meaning the phonetic form gave to Sinn. Mr. Shinn does not deal with the Celtic origin of the name to any extent, although the family Shine was an old family in Ireland long before there is any record of the family in England. And while I have the greatest regard for Mr. Shinn's work, and for his ability as a genealogist, I cannot agree with him in the origin of the name Shine. I am of the opinion that the name is of Celtic origin, and originally of Ireland.

The family did not form a Clan in the early times, except it be "Clan Shane" (see Vol. 1, Hart's Ped., 654), and on that account there appears to be no record of them as a Clan so far as I have been able to learn. The name Shine, as here spelled, is not found much farther back than the 16th century. Before that time it was spelled Shyne, Shene, Sheene, Sheen, Sheyn, Shyn, and still farther back, Segene, Segine, Seigine and O'Seigin. De Courcy, in his "Genealogical History of the Milesians Families of Ireland," published in 1880, on page 31, gives the name "O'Shine" and its ancient name "Siodhachain," meaning "sprightly"

5

Chiefs in Counties Cork, Kerry and Limerick, descendants of Cormac Cas of the Dal Cas Tribe of Milesians. However, I have been unable to confirm De Courcy by any other authority as to the ancient name, or the connection of the family Shine with the Dal Cas Tribe. In Abbe MacGeoghegan's History of Ireland, page 127, among the descendants of Cormac Cas is O'Siodhachain, with the name "Sihan" in parenthesis following it, and indicating that as the more modern spelling of the name, and as the letter "h" was silent the name was pronounced as if spelled Shine, and in all probability this may be De Courcy's authority for the name O'Shine. Mr. Rooney, in his work on Irish Families, page 455, gives a short space to the name and asserts that the ancient name and ancestry to be the same as is found in De Courcy's work, and no doubt was copied from that work.

Rev. P. Wolfe, an eminent Irish scholar and authority on Irish names, of Kilmallock, Ireland, in his work on Irish names and surnames, published in 1906, gives the Irish spelling of the name O'Seigin, and of Sheehan as O'Siodacain and O'Siodeacain. He thinks the name Siodhachain was the ancient name of Sheehan and not Shine, and that its meaning is not "sprightly," but "peaceful," and a diminutive of Siodhach or Sidheach. This meaning is corroborated by the well known traditions attached to the name Sheehan, where the name is most familiar. The writer's grandmother and great grandmother were Sheehans, and in the discussions regarding the names Shine and Sheehan the ancient meaning of the name was frequently spoken of. And it was a tradition of the family, that in ancient times in the wars with the Danes, a counsel of war was held by the chiefs and leaders of the forces as to whether the war should be continued or whether they should make terms of peace. Sheehan, one of the leaders, was for peace, while Shine, another leader, was for a continuance of the war, declaring his sentiments to be "war to the knife's point." It was decided to carry on the war aggressively, and at a banquet given on the occasion, Shine was given the seat of honor at the table, a green baize for his plate, a seat of rushes to sit on, and a silver knife and fork with which to eat. Whether Sheehan's plea for peace was the foundation for the meaning of the name, or whether by it he had earned the name which signified peace it is difficult to say. Whether the names Shine and Sheehan had any connection in early times is not easily determined. The origin of either name is not given in any of the works on names from which it can be satisfactorily determined.

In Hart's Irish pedigrees, among the names of families in Ireland from the 11th to the 16th century, taken from MacDermott's Topographical and Historical map of ancient Ireland, the name O'Sheehan is given in the counties of Kerry, Galway, and were Chiefs in County Limerick, but no pedigree of the family is given. In the appendix to that work the O'Sheehan is given "according to Connellan," as being of the Sept **Dalcassians**, and were Chiefs in the baronies of Conello, County Limerick.

The earliest mention of the name Sheehan that I have been able to find is in the year, A.D., 1290, "Annals of Four Masters."

> "O'Sedaghan, Bishop of Kilmacduagh, died 1290," and is indexed under the name "Sheehan."

In Ware's Bishops the name is spelled Sedacain. In Irish it is given in the Four Masters, O'Secgin. It will be noted that the spelling of the name in Irish is much like the spelling of the name Shine, besides there are other evidences of similarity. The spelling "Sihan" in MacGeoghegan's work, as the short of Siodhachain, might be pronounced Shine or Sheehan. The "h" sound usually followed the letter "S" when it began a name, followed by an "e" or an "i." The letter "g" in a name was generally silent when preceeded by an "e," "i" or "ei," and in Irish a dot over the character "g" indicated that it was silent. Rev. Wolfe, in a letter to the writer, dated August 5, 1910, states:

> "The Irish form of the name O'Seigin is pronounced exactly like the English form O'Shine. In Irish an 's' before 'e' or 'i' is sounded like 'sh' in English. * * * The combination 'eig' is pronounced like 'eye' in English, and the final 'in' like 'in' in English. The whole name then is sounded O'Shyin or O'Shine; 'g' has a sound somewhat like the English 'y.'"

And again in his letter of April 19th, 1909, he says:

> "The name of the Jesuit Father Thomas Sheyn was sometimes written Shine in contemporary documents. Shine seems to have become almost universal after the beginning of the 17th century."

There are some rare instances at the present day where the names Shine and Sheehan are used interchangeably. Hon. Robert E. Matheson, Registrar General, in a work entitled, "Varieties and Synonyms of Surnames and Christian Names in Ireland," published from Dublin, in 1901, gives the names "Sheehan" and "Shine" as used interchangeably in a part of Athlone in the County of Roscommon. Rev. Wolfe, speaking of this, says:

> "As regards the connection with Sheehan, that occurs in the neighborhood of Athlone; it came about in this way. O'Siodacain was anglicized in the 16th century as O'Shiaghane, and here are the different steps by which from that form we reach Shine: O'Sheaghane, O'Sheahane, O'Shihane, O'Shiane, Shiane, Shine. The cases in which this has occurred are so few that I did not think it necessary to put that into my book."

Whether those names had the same origin in ancient times or not will perhaps some day be known. Records may exist that would disclose the fact, but if they do exist they apparently are not known to writers of genealogy so far as I can learn.

But to deal more particularly with the name "Shine," the same author, Rev. Wolfe, writing under date of May 20, 1908, says:

> "Shine is one of our best known Munster surnames, and O'Seigin (pronounced O'Shine) is the Irish form all through the province. In Munster there is no other form. Before surnames were formed, that is, before the 10th and 11th centuries. O'Seigin was a very common personal name. There are seven saints named Seigin in the Martyrology of Donegal. * * * The oldest spelling of the name is Segeni, Segene, Segine, Seigine. Seigin is the modern form. * * * In the Elizabethan records it appears—written according to pronunciation—as O'Sheyne and O'Shine, but it has to be remembered, O'Sheyne of that period had the same sound as the present O'Shine; in other words, that 'ey' in the 16th century form was meant to represent the Irish 'eig.' That is the sound of the modern 'i' as in 'like' or in 'Shine.' O'Heyne, which you mention, is another example. This surname is now nearly always Hynes or Hines. So O'Sheyne has been modernized Shine owing to the change in the

value of the English letters. There is, however, no connection between O'Heyne and O'Sheyne beyond a certain similarity of sound. And I can well understand how they may very easily be confused. O'Seigin in certain positions under the influence of aspiration is pronounced very nearly like O'Heyne. For instance, Mary Shine and Mary Hines would be pronounced, in Irish, Mary Hine and Mary Ine respectively."

The earliest record I can find of the name may be said to be in the year, A.D., 630. However, in Hart's Irish Pedigrees, Vol. 1, page 421, at No. 100 in the Dowling pedigree, about the year 594, we find:

> "Cineth, son of Brandubh, son of Eochaidh, tenth Christian King of Leinster, had a brother named Seicne (or Seigin). And on page 472, where it is spelled Seicin, and spelled Seigin and Seicne, on pages 421, 691 and 692."

The name "Oisin," a traditional poet warrior of the third century, in Ireland, is referred to by Camden, a writer of the twelfth century, as "O'Shin," Vol. 1, Tom Moor's History (foot note).

Mr. Hart, in his work on Irish Pedigrees, book one, page 689, gives the name "Eochardh (Eocha) Sinne," a great great grandson of Brian, eldest brother of the Monarch Niall of the Nine Hostages. And on page 885, he mentions, as one of the ancient Irish Surnames, "Mac Gilla Sinin." And on page 785, the name "Suin" (spelled "Sin" in Mac Geoghegan's History, page 68) as the great great great grandfather of Fiatach Fionn, 45th Monarch of the line of Heremon. And Magee gives the name of Gilshine defending the hill of Tara, in 1797.

These references are given as possibly, of the same name. The Annals of Four Masters of Ireland has reference to four different persons of that name. They are given in the index, Vol. 7, as follows:

> Seghene, Abbot, of Iona—Church founded by. Year 630.
> —— —— died 651.
> Seghene St. Bishop of Ard—Macha, died 686.
> Seghene of Clarach, died 744.

Referring to the subject matter under the years referred to we find this mention made in the year, A.D., 630, Vol. 1, page 251:

> "Segene Abbot of Ia—Coluim Cille founded the church of Rechrainn."
>
> **Note at foot of page**: "Rechrainn, now Ragharee or Rathlin Island, situated off the north coast of the County of Antrim." The Latin form of the name is given as Segienus.

And, on page 293, year A.D., 686:

> "St. Seghene, Bishop of Ard—Mache died. He was from Achadh—Claidhibh."
>
> Note: "Achadh—Claidhibh, situation unknown to the Editor. The Festival of this holy Bishop is marked in O'Cleary's Irish Calendar at 24th of May, and it is added that he died in the year 687, which agrees with the Annals of Ulster."

And, on page ——, year A.D., 744, it reads:

> "Seigeine of Clarach died"

Here we have the same name spelled in several different ways. Under date A.D., 744, we find it Seigeine in the text, and Seghene in the index. Again, we find it Segene and Seghene.

They were prominent in ecclesiastical work in these early times—the scholars, the Abbots and Bishops of the country.

The name appears several times among the martyred saints in the "Martyrology of Donegal," as follows:

> Seighin, son of Fachtna, Abbot of Ia-Coluim Cille, A.D., 651, when he resigned his spirit (p. 217).
> Seighin, son of Ua Cuinn, Abbot of Benchor (p. 243).
> Seighin, Bishop of Ard-Macha, A.D., 687 (he commenced in the year 641 or 644; p. 139).
> Seighin, of Cill-Seighin (p. 25).
> Seighin. The three Clairenechs were Cronan, Bacithin and Seighin (p. 31).
> Seighein—(p. 227).

10

Seighin—(p. 307).

Seghin, Abbot of Ia. This book says that he was a son of Fachtna, and the Saints-Genealogies that he was son of Fiachra, or of Ronan, Segeni, Abbot of Ia, is commemorated on the same day in the Festilogium of the Psalter of Cashel.

The name **Seinchinn** is given in the Four Masters, under date, 1013. He was an anchorite, a religious person of severe self denial. The name appears again in A.D., 1052, as Sinnachain, Patrick's stewart. These names are very similar to those above mentioned. They were also of the clergy and no doubt of the same family.

Then, again, we have the name O'Scingin, mentioned in the Four Masters, in A.D., 1224, as Erenagh of Ardcarne, and in the year 1289, Matthaw Scingin, historian of Ireland. This name is indexed as O'Sgingin, and this is the spelling of the name as written at pages 76 and 77 of "Tribes and Customs of Hy-Fiachrach," where they were mentioned as historians to O'Donnell. And at page 200 of the same work, we find reference to a place named Sighin, and in Irish, spelled Shigin. And on page 497, Sigin, now t-Sigheain in the Parish of Baltinrobe. A river in the southwestern part of Ireland, spelled Shean by some geographers is written **Shine**. In Vol. VI, 2nd series of Cork Historical and Archaeological Journal, at page 149. And **Castleshin**, near Charleville, was an ancient seat of the Fitz-Geralds, Vol. 1, p. 288, Smith's History of the County and City of Cork.

At an early date we find them entering England and Scotland. In 630 A.D., Segene was Abbot of Iona, an island off the coast of Scotland. In 1430, T. Shene was Vicar of Takeley in England, and one hundred years later, John Shene was Vicar of the same place. He is referred to, in Smith's History of Cork—notes from C. & C. M. S., Vol. 1, p. 439—as follows:

"Stanihurst mentions one Sheyn who was educated at Oxford and wrote a treatise **De Republic**, whom Ware considers may have possibly been the same person. Anthony A. Wood mentions one John Sheyn, a graduate of Oxford, whom he considers was author of this work."

In Anthony Wood's Oxonienses Fasti, at pages 46 and 63 he describes this John Sheyne, as an Irishman from Cork, entered Oxford in 1523. In

Holingshed's Chronicles, Vol. VI, p. 64, he is referred to as John Sheine, and in Richard Stanihurst's description of Ireland, written in he refers to him thus:

"Sheine, Scholar, in Oxford and Paris. He wrote De Republic."

Cambridge, Eustace Beverley H. Scl. M. 1894 A. B. 1897. In the records of Oxford the name is given, Sheen or Scheyne, B. A. 1528, Ma. 9th March, 1523-4.

Here we have the spelling, Shene, Sheyn, Sheyne, Sheen, Scheyne and Sheine, and all references are to the same person.

Ireland, once a noted seat of learning, to whose educational institutions those seeking knowledge came from all parts, had, through the devastation of continued warfare, suffered the loss of her high position as an educator, and her sons were obliged to seek institutions of learning in England and France. Many of the Irish entered Oxford, and Cambridge, and on that account, as well as the continuous warfare carried on, caused many to leave Ireland and settle in England and Scotland. Abbots and Bishops and holy men had gone there from Ireland at an early date, and so it was of those of this family name. The spelling of the name seemed to undergo some change from the time we first find them in Oxford. Even the records there show several different spellings of the name of the same person, while writers of the times spelled the name slightly different.

In 1571, Matthew Sheyne entered Oxford. He was a graduate of Peter House, Cambridge. He was Bishop of Cork and Ross in 1572, and died in 1582. He was appointed by Queen Elizabeth. The records of the diocese of Cork and Ross gives the spelling of the name, Seaine (or Sheyne or Shehan). The name is spelled the same in Brady's Records of Cork, Vol. 3, p. 49. His successor, Bishop Lyons, in a petition to the court, designated him as Shehan (see page 28, Brady's Records of Cork, Vol. 3). However, he entered Oxford as Sheyne and graduated from Peter House as Sheyn. Anthony Wood, in his Athenae Oxonienses, Vol. 2, p. 824, writes the name Sheyne, and says he was an Irishman.

In the Chester marriage licenses of England there is the record of a license issued to Thomas Shine and Elizabeth Tey, dated Jan. 29, 1546-7.

In 1590, Martin Sheene of Berkshire, England, matriculated at All Souls College, aged 16 years.

William Sheene, of Oxfordshire, matriculated at Marlon College, Nov. 21, 1595, aged 15. He took the degree of B. A., June, 1600.

William Sheyne, of Cork, was matriculated at St. Mary's Hall, Oxford, Oct. 31, 1600, and took degree of B. & A., in December, same year.

William Sheene, son of James Sheene, of Warwick, matriculated from Magdalen Hall, in April, 1642.

In Hogan's Description of Ireland (1598), p. 290, under Catalogue Ibernorum in Societe, 1609, appears the name, Thomas Sheyn, at Clonmel, 46 yrs., 25 yrs., in society Gradus 3.

In the foregoing we have followed the name down from the 6th century, and it may be observed that the change in the spelling of the name has been very slight. While according to Wolfe, the pronunciation has not changed. We have shown that from a very early date, ancestors of the family had gone to Scotland and England, teaching Christianity and seeking education. We have noticed also some slight change in the spelling of the name from the first records of the name at Oxford and other schools. We will now follow the name for a while in England and Scotland.

CHAPTER III.

We have seen that Shine (Segene), Abbot of Iona, founded a church on the Island of Iona, near Scotland, in the year 630 A.D. We find at a very early date a Loch in Sutherlandshire, Scotland, called Loch Sithein (Gaelic) pronounced Shecun in Gaelic, and Shine in English. The name is frequently written Loch Sine. It is common knowledge that most places take their name from the name of a person and no doubt Loch Shine in Scotland derived its name from the family name "Shine."

We find in Chauncey's "Antiquities of Hertfordshire," Vol. 1, p. 135, that in 1368, one Sheine became owner of a moiety of the manor which afterwards was known as the "Manor of Shine" or Sheine. That in 1417, it was owned by one William Sheine, spelled Cheiny, who changed the spelling of the manor "Sheine" to "Cheynyes," to perpetuate his name under the changed spelling. The "sh" was easily changed to "ch" without any change in the pronunciation. This change no doubt occurred also in Scotland, in Aberdeenshire, where, in 1430, Cheyne was Laird of Esslemont—see Johnston's Scottish Clans. Lang, in his history of Scotland, refers to "The Ancient Norman-Scott House of Cheyne of Aberdeenshire," in 1703. See Vol. 4, Lang's History of Scotland, p. 257. But I have been unable to find any authority for connecting the name with the Normans. The Gaelic spelling of Cheyne was Seagain, and, in my judgment, is purely Celtic.

The earliest record of settlement in England by the family Shine, that we have at hand, is in the 14th century. Chauncey in his Antiquities of Hertfordshire, Vol. 1, p. 135, says:

> "Hundred of Odsey. Coldridg. Hertfordshire: This vill stands towering upon a hill, about a mile N. E. from Ardeley, which the Saxons called Coldridge. The Manor was divided under two lordships by 41 Edward 1 1 1 (1368) one moiety of this Manor came to one, Sheine, from whom it had the adjunct, 'Manor of Sheine,' to distinguish it from the other part."

14

Manning and Bray, in their history of Surrey, say:

> "In the days of Edward II (1313), Philip Burnet held Tuberville Manor in capite as of the manor of Shene by the service of 18£ per annum and suit of court to Shene."

In Ashmole's Antiquities of Berkshire, p. 161, reference is made to a brass plate on a gravestone near the high altar of Shinfield church on which is inscribed the name, "Ellis of Sheynefyeld." And Shingey Hall, and Shenley, two manor houses in Hertford, existed at the time of the Conquest, 1066. Sir Henry Chauncey, Knight and Sergeant at law, thinks they took their name from "some ancient owner, Shen or Shin."

As we have seen, T. Shene was Vicar of Takeley in 1430, and in 1523, John Sheyne, of Cork, was Vicar of Takeley, and in 1600, William Sheyne, of Cork, matriculated at St. Mary's Hall, Oxford.

The following references to the parish records is quoted from Shinn's History of the Shinn family in Europe and America, p. 22:

Parish of Ellough, Suffolk.

2/26/1733   Jeffrey Ely and Dorcas Sheen of Beccles Parish, married.

The following entries show that Shine, Shiene and Sheene were interchangeable in the sixteenth century.

Parish of Birchington, Kent.

10/2/1578   Henricus Shiene married Johanna Staple.
8/25/1579   Joseph Shine, filius Henrici, bap.; ob. 12/30/1579.
9/10/1581   Agnes Shine, filia Henrici, bap.; ob. 11/20/1591.
8/9/1584   John Shiene, filius Henrici, bap.
3/27/1586   Johanna Shine, filia Henrici Shine, bap.
3/29/1591   Eliz., filia Henrici Shine, bap.
1/1/1597   Henricus Shiene, pat. fam. ob.
1/12/1605   Lawrence Whatema married Anna Sheene.

This is a compact history of the married life of Henry Shine, of Birchington, Kent. Of all that he did while living, this is the meager all that is left to history. But it is enough. It shows that he was a dutiful Christian citizen, living in a peaceful, happy home, and dying under the benedictions of the Church.

Parish of Carlton, Suffolk (Sheen, Shean, Shine).

4/30/1702 Davenish Sheane and Elizabeth Bradden married.

2/8/1703 Davenish Sheane, son of Davenish and Elizabeth, bap.

1/14/1714 John Symonds and Mary Sheen, of Kelsale, Stourton, Wilts, married.

11/26/1738 Mary, daughter of Joseph and Ann Shean, of Mere, bap.

2/22/1740 Elizabeth, daughter of Joseph and Ann Shean, of Mere, bap.

6/27/1743 James Shean and Sarah Ricks, of Mere, married.

4/21/1761 William Shine, of South Brewham, and Ann Odbar, married.

These show that many of the name lived at Carlton.

Parish of Ipswich.

12/18/1686 Robt. Curtis married Elizabeth Sheen.

Parish of Lowestaft, Suffolk (Sheen, Sheene).

11/18/1739 Mary, daughter of Henry and Mary Sheen, christened.

5/7/1742 Owen, son of Henry and May Sheene, christened.

8/28/1743 John, son of Henry and May Sheene, christened.

9/18/1745 Henry, son of Henry and May Sheene, christened.

8/4/1747 Robert, son of Henry and May Sheene, buried.

9/25/1748 Rebecca Sheene born. Died same year.

9/29/1749 Kimberry Sheene born. Died same year.

Parish of St. James, Clerkenwell, London.

4/27/1629 Mary Shinn (Sic) buried from John Hand's House.

Parish of St. Duntan's, Stepney, London.

3/6/1697 Samuel Needles married Elizabeth Sheen.

11/18/1718 John V. Francis married Mary Shin.

2/26/1628 George Shinn (Sic) of Wapping, mariner, married Thomassine Grosse.

Parish of Ledbury, Herefordshire

1575 Joan Shynne, a godmother at a christening.

3/16/1557	Margaret Shynne was buried. On same page the same name is written, "Marg. Shyn."
3/5/1565	William Shynne buried. On same page, written "Shyne."

Parish of St. Peters, Cornhill, London.

1/29/1586	Wedding of Jeames Shene, bachelor, waterman sonne of William Shene and Eliz. Brigges maiden, daughter of Harry Brigges.

Parish of St. Martin in the Fields, London.

7/6/1619	William Shene to Jane Wallis.

Parish of Christ's Church, Newgate, London.

1/29/1694	George Sheen buried.

Parish of St. Helens, Worcester.

1628	Isabel, wife of Thomas Shine, buried.

In advertisements of London papers, seeking claimants to fortunes, George and Henry Sheen are requested to make their whereabouts known; a little lower down the same request is made of George and Henry Shinn. Similar calls are made for John, William, Susannah, Samuel and Thomas Sheen or Shinn.

Westminster Abbey Register.

5/19/1565	James, son of Christopher Sheene, one of the bell ringers of the Abbey, buried in the Cloisters. The father, Christopher, is mentioned in the Chapter Book, 12/11/1660.

These exhaust my printed references and show not only the varied spellings, but point to Suffolk and Kent as the home of the family. Through the kindness of a friend, Mr. W. G. Stockley, Head Master of Mildenhall School, Suffolk, England, I am enabled to supplement these printed registers by numerous others, which he had gathered from various parishes in Herts, Essex, Norfolk and Suffolk.

Parish of Mildenhall, Suffolk.

This register is very old; one of the oldest extant. It was copied from an older one in 1662, and the following note appended:

"Although this register will be found very imperfect by reason of the great division and confusion of these times until the year 1662, yet I thought it more than expedient to set down what names......(not without great difficulty)......and do now proceed in order. May 20, 1662, J. O. Watson, Vicar."

The dotted lines in the certificate are illegible, says Mr. Stockley.

Extracts from this Register. (Shene, Sheene, Sheen, Shine, Shyn, Shyne, Shin.)

Marriages.

June, 1578.	Thomas Shene and J—— Bonet.
June, 1588.	John Sheene and Anne Che——
July, 1589.	Thomas Sheene and Maria Corkett.
May, 1611.	Thomas Wing and L—— Shene.
Jan., 1632.	John Sheene and Ann Rolfe.
Sept. 9, 1639.	John Avis and Elizabeth Shyn.

These complete the list of Mildenhall marriages from 1578 to 1671, a period of ninety-three years. They give us the marriage date of John Sheene and Ann Rolfe. This Ann was a descendant of an ancient family of Ralfs or Rolfs in Norfolk. Mildenhall was settled on Sir John Fitz Ralf in 1402. Another descendant of the same family formed an alliance in Virginia with the famous Indian princess, Pocahontas.

Births and Baptisms.

July, 1588.	John Sheene, son of John Sheene, baptized.
Sept., 1589.	Thomas Sheene, son of John Sheene, baptized.
April, 1590.	Anne, daughter of Thomas Sheene, baptized.
Nov., 1592.	Nicholas, son of John Sheene, baptized.
Oct., 1595.	Richard, son of John Sheene, baptized.
Oct., 1598.	William, son of John Sheene, baptized.
Feb., 1604.	Francis, son of John Sheene, baptized.
Sept., 1633.	Rachel, daughter of John Sheene, baptized.
Oct., 1637.	Richard, son of Richard Sheene, baptized.

March, 1637.	John, son of William Sheene, baptized.
March, 1638.	John, son of John Shyn, baptized.
Aug., 1640.	James, son of William Sheen, baptized.
Nov., 1640.	John, son of John Sheen, baptized.
Sept., 1640.	William, son of Richard Sheen, baptized.
Oct. 18, 1646	Catherine, daughter of John Shin, baptized.
Feb. 2, 1663.	Elizabeth, daughter of John Shin, baptized.
July 22, 1666.	John, son of John Shin, baptized.
March 9, 1669.	Hannah, daughter of John Shin, baptized.
Feb. 4, 1671.	Hannah, daughter of John Shin, baptized.

Burials.

May, 1636.	Francis Shyne buried.
May, 1590.	Anne, daughter of Thomas Sheen, buried.
Oct., 1607.	John Shene, son of John Sheene, buried.
Jan., 1610.	Thomas Sheen buried.
Feb., 1617.	Widow Shine buried.
Feb. 20, 1638.	Richard Shyn buried.
March 30, 1639.	John, son of John Shyne, buried.
July 24, 1644.	William, son of John Shyne, buried.
Aug. 19, 1662.	Rachel, daughter of John Shin, buried.
Jan. 11, 1664.	John Shin buried.
July 5, 1664.	John, son of John Shin, buried.
Jan. 20, 1669.	John, son of John Shin, deceased, buried.
Aug. 27, 1670.	Hannah, daughter of John Shin, buried.
Sept. 9, 1670.	Amy Shin, widow, buried.

Parish of Little Fransham (Shene).

1610.	Ed. Shene, rector.
1617.	Elizabeth, daughter of Ed. Shene, baptized.
1623.	Lucas, son of Ed. Shene, baptized.
1624.	Henry, son of Henry Shene, baptized.
1627.	Anne, daughter of Henry Shene, baptized.
1629.	Elizabeth, daughter of Henry Shene, baptized.

1632. Edward, son of Henry Shene, baptized.

1641. Mary, daughter of John and Margret Shene, baptized.

1647. John, son of Joh Shene, baptized.

1660. Anne, daughter of Ed. Shene, baptized.

1665. Marie, daughter of Ed, Shene, baptized.

Parish of Freckenham (Sheene).

1551. ———, daughter of Francis Sheene, baptized.

1564. Mary, daughter of Francis Sheene, baptized.

1593. Clement, son of John Sheene, baptized, Nov. 24.

1608. Anne, daughter of John Sheene, baptized.

1610. Margaret, daughter of John Sheen, baptized.

1614. John and Nicholas, sons of John Sheene, baptized.

1614. John, son of John Sheene, buried.

1615. Frances, daughter of John Sheene, baptized.

1615. Nicholas, son of John Sheene, buried.

1616. Elizabeth, daughter of Francis Sheene, baptized.

1617. Anne, wife of John Sheene, buried.

1618. Francis, son of Francis Sheene, baptized.

1619. Marie married John Sheene.

1619. ———, son of Sheene, baptized.

1620. Marie, wife of John Sheene, buried.

1621. John, wid., married Marie Spatkes.

1621. Anne, daughter of John Sheene, baptized.

1623. John, son of Francis Sheene, baptized.

1627. Thomas, son of Francis Sheene, baptized.

1628. Marie, wife of John Sheene, buried.

1630. Thomas, son of John Sheene, baptized.

1630. Thomas, son of John Sheene, buried.

1631. Joane, wife of Francis Sheene, buried.

1631. John, son of Francis Sheene, buried.

1642. Anne, daughter of William Sheene, baptized.

1645. Mary, daughter of William Sheene, baptized.

1633. John, son of Francis Sheene, buried.

EXTRACTS FROM J. J. MURKETT'S COLLECTION CONCERNING THE MANORIAL FAMILIES OF SUFFOLK.

"Family of Shene, Shine, Shinn, etc.—Gleanings.

"Will of Robt. Blosse, of Roydon, Suffolk, P. C. C. 70, Leicester, 1589. "To John Shinne, sonne of John Shyne, my house called, Haggerel, after the decease of Amiable, my wife."

"Will of Edward Sheene of Wymondham, Norfolk, Gent., proved 1658. Had son, Jermyn Shene. Lands in Suffolk, P. C. C. Wooten 349."

"Will of Thomas Shene of Stowmarket, Worsted Weaver; proved 1711. P. C. C. Young 91."

"Will of Alice Blackbye of Multou, Suffolk, 1565; 24th of April. P. C. C. 21, Morrison & Grimes. She did give to Jane Mynt of Freckenham, her daughter; to Agnes Shynne, her daughter; and her residence to Thomas Blackbie, her son and executor. Probate 6/24/1565 to Thos. Blackbie, the son."

"Will of Edward Sheene of Wymondham, in Norfolk, Gent. P. C. C. 2/11/1657. To be buried in the church. To Dorothy, my wife, houses and lands in Norfolk, and also at Hoxene, in Suffolk, for life. Our three children, Jermyn Sheene, my only sonne; Annie Sheene, eldest d.; Sarah Sheene, youngest d. Wife, executrix. Probate 5/27/1658."

This Edward was son of the Edward Sheen who was rector of Little Fransham, in 1610; married Dorothy, daughter of Sir Thomas Jermyn, as the next will shows.

"Will of Thos. Jermyn, Esq., of West Tofts in Norfolk, 11/5/1656. P. C. C. 172 Wooten. My sonne, John Jermyn, etc.; my grandchild, Jermyn Shene, when 18; Mrs. Dorothy Shene, mother of said Jermyn Shene. etc."

"Will, P. C. C. 39 Wood, of Willie Haywards, of Roydon, Suffolk, 1611. To my grandchildren, Thos. Bridge, John Bridge, Anna Browne, the wife of Willie Brown, and Ann Shinne, the wife of George Shinn, my daughter, Marian Knopper, of Newton, etc."

ADDITIONAL MATTER FROM ENGLISH PARISH RECORDS.

Fordham Register.

(Shinne-Shinn.)

1649. Francis Shinne m. Anne Hynds—June.

1654. Richard, son of Francis, d.—April.

1656. Francis, wid., m. Anne Baker (?) of Soham.

1660. Elizabeth, d., of John Shinne, bap.—June.

1662. Mary, D. of John Shinne, bap.—March.

1676. Phillip Hinson m. Margaret Shinn—September.

Sutton Register.

(Shyn.)

1660. William, son of John Shyn, bap. Aug. 10.

1678. Thomas, son of John Shyn, Jr., and Anne, bap. April 14.

1679. Margaret, d. of John Shyn, Jr., and Anne, bap.

1683. Anne, d. of John Shyn, Jr., and Anne, bap.

1684. William, son of John Shyn, Jr., and Anne, bap.

1686. John, son of John Shyn, Jr., and Anne, bap.

Marriages.

1656. John Shin m. Alice Frost.

1659. John Shin m. Bridget Papper.

1663. John Sheen m. Ann Fremont.

1677. John Shinn m. Ann Phillips.

The above were furnished by Mr. W. G. Stockley, in letter dated May 27th, 1903."

It will be observed that in England there is a tendency to drop the final "e," and we frequently find the name spelled Shyn, Shin and Shinn, and thus was originated the family name Shinn.

CHAPTER IV.

In Ireland the name was sometimes spelled Shyne and sometimes Shine, and in later times almost invariably Shine. As we have seen, the "y" was used in the 15th and 16th centuries. We find John Sheine, also spelled Sheyne, at Oxford, in 1523. Matthew Sheyne, Bishop of Cork, in 1572. Thomas Sheyn at Clonmel in 1598. William Sheyne of Cork at Oxford in 1600.

The Fiants of Elizabeth gives the following:

A.D., 1584.	Pardon to Tho. Oge. O'Shene of Iveaghe (Co. Cork) Kern. F. E. 4467.
A.D., 1584.	Pardon to Owen O'Sheyne McConoghor, householder in Co. Cork. F. E. 4533.
A.D., 1585-6.	Pardon to Owen McConnoghor O'Sheine, of Lohirt (Co. Cork), yeoman, F. E. 4814.
A.D., 1588.	Pardon to Owen O'Sheyne McConnoghor, of Toughor (Co. Kerry), F. E. 5226.
A.D., 1590.	Pardon to William Sheyne, of Liksnawe, Co. Kerry, F. E. 5457.
A.D., 1601.	Pardon to Philip McTeig O'Sheine, of Castle McAwliffe (Co. Cork). F. E. 6558.
A.D., 1601.	Pardon to William O'Sheyne, of Dromagh (Co. Cork), yeoman. F. E. 6566.
A.D., 1602-3.	Pardon to John McTho Oge O'Sheyne, of Glannyfunhy (Co. Cork), yeoman. F. E. 6762.

And although in some instances the name is to this day spelled "Shyne," it is most generally spelled "Shine." The earliest instance I can find of the name being spelled "Shine" is in 1579, in the Parish of Birchington, Kent.

"8/25/1579. Joseph Shine Auis Henrici baptized."

In the baptismal records of this family the name is spelled both "Shine" and "Sheine."

In 1633, we find a marriage license issued to Peter De La Shine and Sarah Skipwith, in the diocese of Cork and Ross, and in 1728, Richard Shine and Mary Stephens.

There is a tombstone in the chapel at Ballyhea cemetery, near Charleville, in Co. Cork, on which is the following inscription:

> "Lord have mercy on the soul of Thomas Shine, who died
> Feb. 14, 1769, age 66 years."

The Shine family appears to have settled in the counties of Cork, Limerick and Kerry. Rev. Wolfe, writing in 1908, says the name "Shine" is one of the best known Munster surnames.

In 1890, Robert E. Matheson, Register General of Marriages, Births and Deaths in Ireland, in a report, gives the following interesting data relative to the births of children of the name Shine. In 1890, there were 26 births, divided as follows: 2 in Leinster, 21 in Munster, 3 in Connought, of which 12 were in the County of Cork.

Registry of baptisms taken from Registry Books kept at Ballyclough, Parochial House, by me.

Patrick Ring, C. C.,
Ballyclough.

The Name Shine, etc.

1808

Date	Child	Parents	Sponsors
March 13th	Catherine	Dennis Shine	John Connelan
		Mary Fitzpatrick	
Oct. 24th	Ellen	John Shine	William Reilly
		Mary Neill	Mary Reilly

1809

Date	Child	Parents	Sponsors
Nov. 27th	John	John Shine	Jerry Fitzpatrick
		Norry Coll	Kate Canty

Nov. 27th	Johanna	John Shine Norry Coll	Same sponsors

1810

May 11th	Margaret	Dennis Shine Marry Fitzpatrick	Thomas Hennessy Julia Murphy

1811

May 24th	Jane	Richard Keeffe Judith Shine	Ellen Roche Maurice Keeffe
Dec. 29th	John	John Shine Jane Kavanaugh	John Reilly Mary Cavanagh

1814

April 1st	Catherine	John Shine Jane Cavanagh	John Murphy Norry Reilly
April 11th	Catherine	John Shine Norry Callaghan	Cornelius Drea Jane Lyne

1815

November 19th	Michael	John Shine Norry Callaghan	Timothy Callaghan Michael Riordan

1816

December 23rd	Ellen	John Shine Johannah Cavanagh	Thomas Tivomey Mary Sullivan

1817

July 26th	Ellen	Thomas Shine Ellen Mahony	Dennis Leahy Ellen Thomson
October 6th	Honora	Dennis Shine Catherine Dennehy	John Buckley Catherine Connell

1818

May 3rd	Mary	Edmond Shine	James Sheehan
		Mary Flynn	Johanna Shine
May 17th	Dennis	John Shine	John Brawen
		Horona Callaghan	Catherine Brown
June 15th	Margaret	Patrick Mulcahy	William Brien
		Catherine Shine	Bridget Shine

1819

January 10th	Mary	Denis Leahy	Denis Daley
		Mary Shine	Johanna Cronin
April 1st	John	Thomas Shine	James Sheehan
		Abira Cronin	Mary Cronin
December 9th	Ellen	Thomas Shine	Matt Ring
		Ellen Mahony	Kate Ronan

1820

March 25th	Mary	Cornelius Shine	David Linahan
		Johanna Sheehan	Mary Purdon
October 13th	David	Thomas Shine	Peter Correll
		Elizabeth Cremir	Margaret Shine
December 19th	Johanna	Edmond Shine	James Duckett
		Mary Flynn	Mary Flynn

1821

March 12th	Edmond	David Shine	Edmond Murphy
		Johanna Leary	Mary Cavanagh
May 18th	Catherine	Patrick Mahony	Laurance Brien
		Catherine Shine	Mary Begly
December 28th	Catherine	John Shine	David Begly
		Mary Sheehan	Margaret Sheehan

1822

March 4th	(Not given)	Deniis Connor	Cornelis Connor
		Mary Shine	—— Connor

April 13th	John	Timothy Shine	Robb Broke
		Anne Farrant	Ellen Barrett
October 25th	William	Thomas Shine	Owen Cremin
		Betty Cronin	Catherine Sullivan
December 21st	Mary	Denis Shine	Thomas Mahony
		Ellen Donoghue	Ellen Scanlan

1823

October 1st	John	Thomas Shine	Dennis Shine
		Mary Sheehan	Margaret Kennedy

1824

February 22nd	Mary	John Shine	Jerry Galvin
		Kate Galvin	Mary Galvin
February 29th	James	Thomas Shine	Thado Finn
		Ellen Shea	Judy McAuliffe
April 13th	Biddy	James Shine	Jerry Hartnett
		Nancey Tarrant	Catherine Philpot
May 31st	Betty	Dennis Connor	Patrick Shine
		Mary Shine	Mary Philpot

1825

February 26th	Johanna	John Shine	Timothy Murphy
		Marry Buckley	Johanna Brien
May 3rd	Timothy	Michael Leahy	Timothy Crean
		Kate Shine	Margaret Murphy
August 2nd	Jerry	Jerry Murphy	James Connell
		Anne Shine	Margaret Sheehan
August 21st	Daniel	Thomas Shine	Thomas Beecher
		Mary Sheehan	Ellen Sheehan
November 12th	Johanna	Dennis Connor	Thomas Shine
		Mary Shine	Anne Connor

1826

1827

January 4th	Andrew	Andy Sheehan	Timothy Keffee
		Mary Shine	Mary Shine
March 5th	Mary	John Shine	Patrick Guinee
		Mary Buckley	Margaret Murphy

1828

January 11th	Margaret	Thomas Shine	Patrick Brown
		Mary Sheehan	Johanna Sheehan
April 19th	Cornelius	Dennis Connors	Patrick McCarty
		Mary Shine	Honoria Connors

1829

| January 14th | Eliza | Thomas Shine | Philip Moloney |
| | | Mary Sheehan | Ellen McAuliffe |

1830

| January 24th | David | John Shine | Michael Lombard |
| | | Mary Buckley | Ellen Power |

1831

| December 23rd | James | Michael Lombard | John Crowley |
| | | Ellen Shine | Honoria Sheehan |

1834

| March 16th | Johanna | Michael Lombard | Thomas Twomey |
| | | Ellen Shine | Mary Sheehan |

1835

1836

| August 19th | Ellen | Thomas Shine | Daniel Sheehan |
| | | Mary Sheehan | Mary Harrigan |

1837

1838

April 15th	Jermiah	Cornelius Connors	Johanna Sheehan
		Johanna Shine	Ellen Connors
November 4th	John	Michael Shine	Patrick Fitzgerald
		Mary Fitzgerald	Honoria Callaghan

1839—none

1840

January 19th	John	Cornelius Sheehan	John Shine
		Catherine Shine	Mary Power
December 25th	Anne	Cornelius Shine	John Reilly
		Jane Keeffe	Honora Flynn

1841

January 1st	Eleanor	Bartholomew Higgins	Timothy Shine
		Julia Shine	Mary Mahony
May 12th	Cornelius	Cornelius Shine	Robert Britt
		Betty ——	—— ——
December 17th	John	Bartholomew Higgins	Dennis Shine
		Julia Shine	Mary Barrett

1842

May 22nd	Thomas	Cornelius Sheehan	Maurice Sheehan
		Catherine Shine	Honora Regan
October 8th	Mary	Daniel Corcoran	Bartholomew Daley
		Ellen Shine	Ellen Daley

1843—1844—none

1845

February 17th	Johanna	John Shine	Richard Cavanaugh
		Johanna Searrel	John Shine

| September 21st | Cornelius | Cornelius Sheehan | John Power |
| | | Catherine Shine | Catherine Twomery |

P.S.—This completes the registry of baptisms entered in books kept here in which the name Shine occurs, from January, 1808, to December, 1845.

Dated: November 6th, 1901.

P. Ring.

The baptismal records at Charleville, Co. Cork, Ireland, contain the following references, furnished by Rev. P. J. Callaghan:

Date	Child	Parents
September 30th, 1827	Catherine	John Shine
		Mary Anne Kirby
August 5th, 1828	Eliza	Denis Shine
		Honora Power
March 22nd, 1829	Patrick	Michael Shine
		Mary (or Margaret) Hickey
January 9th, 1831	Kate	Denis Shine
		Honora Power
December 30th, 1832	John	Michael Shine
		Mary (or Margaret) Hickey
March 22nd, 1835	Mary	Denis Shine
		Honora Power
May 16th, 1837	William	Denis Shine
		Honora Power
August 11th, 1839	Thomas	Denis Shine
		Honora Power

The records of the Public Record Office at Dublin, under Prerogative Index to Wills, gives the following reference to wills and date of probate:

Katherine Shine, Macroom	1732
William Shine, Capt. in General Moyles Regiment on foot	1739
Cornelius Shine, Newcastly, Co. Limerick, Gent.	1775
Richard Shine (or Shien) of Passage, Co. Cork	1777
Timothy Shine, Cooleen, Cork Co.	1777
Dennis Shine, Mount Infant, Cork	1798

Jonathan Shine, Cork	1798
Dennis Shine, Cork	1799
Dennis Shine, Rath Reale, Co. Limerick, mason	1810
William Shine, Clash, Co. Cork	1819
Roger Shine, Ballymacresse, Co. Limerick	1825
William Shine, Dame Street, Dublin, cloth merchant	1847
Timothy Shine, Glass Kauline, Cork, farmer	1848
William Shine, Bandon, Cork Co.	1849
Bartholomew Shine, Talleland, Co. Cork	1849
Jeremiah Shine, Edwardstown & Cooly Henan House, Limerick	1850

CHAPTER V.

There are several families of the name Shine still living in Ireland.
J. Hickman Shine, residing at Ballymacresse, Ballymeety, in the County of
Limerick, represents the 4th generation residing at that place, the family
having settled there in 1775. This family is related to Colonel Harrison, of
Castle Harrison, near Charleville. In 1908, the writer had the pleasure of
visiting with Colonel Harrison, at his home—Castle Harrison, and enjoyed
very much a few hours' visit with him. Colonel Harrison served in the Boer
war, and for exceptional service there was raised to the rank of colonel. The
late Jeremiah Shine, father of J. Hickman Shine, was married at Castle
Harrison to a cousin of Colonel Harrison, and on his death, in 1901, his son,
the present proprietor of his estate in Limerick and Clare, who was in the
United States, returned to Ireland to take charge of the estate. Mr. Shine is of
the impression that his family came originally from County of Kerry. Their
family crest is—"The Sun surrounded by seven stars," with the French
motto—

> "Briler Sans Bruler—est mon espoir," and means:
> "Shine without burning."

They are possibly descendants of Thomas Shine of Cooleen, hereinafter
mentioned.

Patrick Shine, living, in 1908, about one mile from Tarbert, in the
County Kerry, on a fine estate. He formerly lived in the Townland of Kilbaha,
in the County Kerry, about five miles from Listowell. He had been a teacher
in the schools of that place for many years, a scholarly gentleman of the old
class. In physique he was of more than ordinary height and well proportioned.
He settled where he now lives—Carhoona, Tarbert, Co. Kerry—in 1892. His
grandfather's name was Cornelius Shine and he came from County Limerick
and settled at Kilbaha Newtownsands, Co. Kerry, where he took a farm of a
gentleman of the name of Wall; while his two brothers settled in Dirreen
Parish of Athea, Co. Limerick. This Cornelius Shine had three sons: Daniel

(father of the present Patrick Shine), John and Cornelius. Daniel Shine had four sons: Cornelius, who lives at Kilbaha, on the old farm where the grandfather, Cornelius, settled, and after him his son, Daniel. John, now deceased, resided on a farm at Ahanagran Parish at Ballylongford. Patrick Shine, of Carhoona Tarbert, and William, now deceased, who was Superior General of the Presentation Monks in Cork City.

SHINES OF COOLEEN—BALLYMICHAEL.

A family of Shines lived at Cooleen, near Kilbarry, in County Cork, prior to 1800. Some of the old settlers think some of them settled near Kilmallock, Co. Limerick. One of them, Daniel Shine, moved to Ballymichael, Parish of Kilmurray, County Cork, sometime before 1798. He operated a flouring mill there. He went to America in about the year 1819. This family of Shines were related by marriage to the Buckleys, of Kilbarry, Co. Cork. Michael Buckley living in 1908. His father, Michael Buckley, had an uncle, Timothy Buckley, who married, in England, a lady of property. They sold the property and went to America. His wife and children died soon after. He returned to Ireland about the year 1818, to take his nephew, Michael Buckley, with him to America. Michael Buckley preferred staying at Inchigeela, where he had settled, and Timothy Buckley took with him one of the Shines and settled in Philadelphia, and his property finally went to Shine, who came to America with him. This Timothy Buckley had four sisters—Margaret, Mary, Honora and Ellen; one of them was the mother of these Shines. This information was furnished by the late Michael Buckley, Sr., and by the present Michael Buckley, of Kilbarry, Co. Cork. But whether the Shine that accompanied Buckley to America was the Daniel Shine of Ballymichael or not, I could not learn. He was said to be a very large man and possessed of great physical strength and prowess.

SHINES OF MALLOW—BALLYCLOUGH—COOLEEN.

1. Thomas Shine.

Thomas Shine lived in Cooleen (a parish), in the southern part of the County Limerick. Whether the family had resided in that vicinity for several generations or not we have been unable to learn. It is claimed by descendants of the family that this Thomas Shine was living there (about the year 1775, and as we are unable to trace back farther with any degree of certainty, we will designate him as the founder of this branch of the family Shine. He had three sons, Daniel, John and Thomas.

2. Daniel Shine.

It is believed that Daniel Shine settled at Ballymichael, in the Parish of Kilmurry, and engaged in the flouring mill business, and from all accounts may be the Daniel Shine referred to in the previous chapter.

3. Thomas Shine.

Thomas Shine remained in Limerick county and engaged in farming there. He held a large estate and was said to be a prosperous farmer. It is probable that the Shine family now at Ballymacreese, Co. Limerick, and the New York family of Shine, coming from Charleville, are descendants of him.

4. John Shine.

John Shine, son of Thomas Shine, left Cooleen about the year 1775, and settled at Ballyclough, near Mallow. It is not definitely known the order of birth of these three sons, but Thomas is said to be the youngest brother. It is not known what business their father, Thomas Shine, of Cooleen, was engaged in, but in all probability the flouring mill business. We do know, however, that when his son, John, settled at Ballyclough, he engaged in that business, and his son, Daniel, engaged in the same business at Ballymichael.

John Shine was born about the year 1750, and died about the year 1835; was buried at Ballyhea cemetery, near Charleville. It seems that this was the family burial place. Charleville is situated in Cork county and close to the county line dividing County of Cork and County Limerick. Cooleen parish was in Limerick County, close to the line and near Charleville. Ballyhea cemetery is about two miles out from Charleville. Ballyclough is about four miles from Mallow and about fifteen miles from Charleville. Perhaps twelve miles from the cemetery, yet the burials from Ballyclough were made at this cemetery. There is a tomb stone still standing there inside the walls of the old chapel in the cemetery, bearing this inscription:

"Lord have mercy on the soul of Thomas Shine, who died February 14, 1769; aged 66 years."

This may have been the father or grandfather of Thomas Shine first above mentioned.

John Shine soon after settling in Ballyclough, acquired lands there and erected a stone flouring mill operated by a water wheel. The building, although not used for that purpose for upwards of sixty years, still stands (in the year 1908) in a fairly good state of preservation. The mill pond is still there, and the water wheel is in place. John Shine married Catherine Sheehan and had nine children, three sons and six daughters:

5.	(1)	Margaret, born about 1782.
6.	(2)	Catherine, born about 1785.
7.	(3)	Bridget, born about 1787.
8.	(4)	Mary, born about 1789.
9.	(5)	Johana, born about 1791; never married; lived at Mallow.
10.	(6)	Ellen, born about 1794; never married.
11.	(7)	Thomas, born about 1796; died at Ballyclough, about 1837.
12.	(8)	John, born about 1798; died at New York, about 1864.
13.	(9)	Daniel, born about 1800; died at New York, about 1856.

In about the year 1820, he sold the mill to a company named Haines Smith, and reserved the residence and grounds. The company erected a large seven-story mill near the Shine mill, and John Shine continued as superintendent of both these mills. The large mill has long since been taken down, but the foundation may yet be seen where it stood. After his death, his wife, Catherine Shine, continued to occupy the residence until the time of her death, about the year 1839. The house was then occupied by her daughter, Ellen, until her death, about the year 1840. Then the place was occupied by John Moloney and his wife, Catherine Shine, a daughter of John Shine (No. 8) and Mary Anne Kirby, until about the year 1870, when Catherine Shine Moloney transferred whatever right she claimed to Mr. Coots, the landlord who owned lands all around that neighborhood. The title to this property, on the death of John Shine, passed to his son, Thomas, and through him to his son, John Shine, of Michigan.

Catherine Sheehan, wife of John Shine, had a sister, Elizabeth, who married William Lillis, of Charleville, of whom hereafter. Of the children of John Shine and Catherine Sheehan, one of the daughters married a man by the name of Wagner; another married a Mr. Murphy and lived at Mallow; they had a son, Dean Murphy. Another married a Mr. Roach and lived at Cork.

11. Thomas Shine (2); John Shine (1).

Thomas Shine was the eldest son of John Shine and Catherine Sheehan. He was named after his grandfather, Thomas Shine, of Cooleen. He married Mary Sheehan (no relation to his mother, Catherine Sheehan), and resided at Ballyclough, Mallow, and they had two sons and five daughters, namely:

14. (1) Catherine, born Dec., 1821; m. Thomas Kiley; d. Jan. 16, 1911.
15. (2) John, born Sept. 27, 1823; m. Catherine Moore; d. Feby. 4, 1902.
16. (3) Daniel, born Aug., 1825; d. June, 1826.
17. (4) Margaret, born Jan., 1828; d. in infancy.
18. (5) Eliza, born Dec. 25, 1828; m. Thomas Francis Gallagher; d. March 25, 1909.
19. (6) Mary, born Sept., 1830; m. Joh Starr; d. Nov. 27, 1915.
20. (7) Ellen, born Aug., 1836; m. William King; d. May 14, 1910.

Thomas Shine died at Ballyclough, in about the year 1837. His only surviving son, John, after finishing his education, spent several years in England and Wales, and finally settled in Michigan, of whom hereafter. In 1840, his widow, Mary Sheehan Shine, and four daughters, Catherine, Eliza, Mary and Ellen, sailed for America, from Queenstown, and after a seven weeks rough and tempestuous voyage, landed at Quebec, Canada. Mrs. Shine died at Quebec that same year. She had three sisters and two brothers, Catherine Sheehan Keaf, Norah Sheehan Waters, Margaret Mahaney, William Sheehan and John Sheehan. Only one of them came to America, I believe. It is claimed that John Sheehan came to America; he was not married.

12. John Shine (1); John Shine (2).

John Shine, second eldest son of John Shine and Catherine Sheehan, married Mary Anne Kirby, of Charleville. Her father died and her mother married a Mr. David Kelley, who kept a hotel in Charleville at what was known as Goggins Corners. Mary Anne Kirby's dower, when she married John Shine, was seven hundred pounds sterling. John Shine engaged in the mercantile business at Charleville. He was reputed to have been very wealthy; at one time there were over fifty clerks employed about his store. There were three children born of that marriage:

21.   (1)   Sarah, born ——; never married.
22.   (2)   John, born ——; died a young man.
23.   (3)   Catherine, born Sept., 1827; m. John Moloney—living in Chicago in 1909.

Mary Anne Kirby, wife of John Shine, died, and he married again, but to whom I have been unable to learn. There were no children of this second marriage so far as I can learn. He left Ireland about the year 1839, and went to New York, where he was connected with the mercantile house of A. T. Stewart. It was reported that about the year 1841, while about to return to Ireland, he was killed, but I have been unable to obtain definite information of it. It was also said that his daughter, Sarah, died at a convent in New York.

13. Daniel Shine (2); John Shine (1).

Daniel Shine, the third son of John Shine and Catherine Sheehan, never married so far as known. When a boy or young man, he lived most of the time with his aunt, Elizabeth Lillis, at Charleville. He engaged in the leather business at Charleville. This was sometime between the years 1830 and 1843. He was also, for a time, superintendent over the currier department of the business for his Aunt Lillis. He left Ireland about the year—and went to New York. The last account of him was from New Jersey. He was mentioned as a legatee in the will of Elizabeth Lillis.

Elizabeth Lillis.

Elizabeth Lillis was a sister of Catherine Sheehan, wife of John Shine. She married William Lillis, of Charleville; she had two children, a son and daughter; her son died a young man, and her daughter, Margaret, married Cahill and had no children. Elizabeth Lillis was engaged in the tanning business and was possessed of several houses in Charleville. She became wealthy. She had no brothers and only one sister, Catherine Sheehan Shine, so far as known. Her male heirs were the children of her sister, Catherine, and as the oldest son was heir to the father's estate, Thomas Shine, the eldest son of Catherine Sheehan, would be the nearest male heir of Elizabeth Lillis, and his son, John, would succeed him. It was the understanding among those interested that the greater part of the estate of Elizabeth Lillis would go to John Shine, son of Thomas Shine and Mary Sheehan, as the lawful heir of Elizabeth Lillis. She made her will in October, 1835, and died soon after. See appendix for copy of the will. Margaret Cahill and her husband continued to live at Charleville for several years. They finally left Charleville and moved to Ballynoe, near Queenstown. Margaret Cahill died without issue, and believing that the family of Thomas Shine was lost at sea, John Shine was sent for to take possession of the Charleville property and the Shine homestead at Ballyclough, but he died when about to leave New York for Queenstown. It was reported he was killed. On leaving Charleville, Cahill sold his interest in the property to Mr. Edward Haines, of Mallow, who worked the tan yard for years. The place fell into the hands of Mr. Quinn. The National Bank got hold of it and sold it to Mr. Kelliher, who turned the tannery building into a coal store. It was in 1908 used as a creamery. About the year 1870, Catherine Shine Moloney sold her claim to the old Shine homestead to Mr. Coote, of Bearforest, near Mallow. The dwelling was not standing in 1908.

Other persons of the name "Shine," residing in Ireland:

24. Major J. M. Shine, A. M. S. Barricks, Cahir, Ireland. Major Shine was a member of the Cork Historical and Archaeological Society of Cork.
25. Rev. W. P. Shine, residing in Cork, in 1908.
26. Timothy Shine, residing at 44 College Road, Cork, in 1908.
27. James Shine, residing at Blossomfort, Ballyclough Mallow, in 1908.
28. John Shine, residing at Knockshehy Meelin (New-market), in 1908.

38

29. Jerome Shine, residing at Bandon, 1908.
30. Michael Shine, residing at Kanturk, in 1908.
31. James P. Shine, residing at New Market, in 1908.
32. James Shine, residing at Coolyhenan, Limerick Co., in 1908. And many others whose names I have been unable to get.

These families are, no doubt, all related to the same Shine family, but I have been unable to get any data to establish their relations.

THE SHINE FAMILY IN AMERICA.

CHAPTER VI.

The earliest settlement of the family Shine in America, so far as I can learn, was in the States of Massachusetts, North Carolina and Virginia. In the genealogical register of Massachusetts is the name, John Shine, in 1635, and with the remark: "the name is strange." Three brothers came from Dublin, Ireland, and settled in North Carolina early in the 18th century, and about the year 1710. They were:

33. Daniel Shine.
34. Francis Shine.
35. James or John Shine.

I am indebted to Mr. Junius Augustus Shine, of Faison N. C., for this information. From an old writing found among his father's papers, dated September 12, 1783, the following is reproduced:

(Copy.)

North Carolina Nuos Record, May the 15th, 1715—D. Shine and Elizabeth Greene were married.

Children.

36.	(1)	Hannah Shine, born July 16, 1718.
37.	(2)	Elizabeth Shine, born February 19, 1721.
38.	(3)	Mary Shine, born July 11, 1724.
39.	(4)	John Shine, born Nov. 25, 1725.
40.	(5)	Mary Shine, born Dec. 21, 1727.
41.	(6)	Daniel Shine, born May 10, 1729.
42.	(7)	James Shine, born January 9, 1731.
43.	(8)	Sarah Shine, born February 7, 1732.
44.	(9)	Thomas Shine, born Oct. 1, 1736.

45. (10) Francis Shine, born June, 1739.
46. (11) William Shine, born March 25, 1741.

A true list of the ages, Daniel Shine, deceased, his children and his son, John Shine, and the time of marriage of both.

The Ages of Daniel Shine's Children.

John Shine and Sarah Shelweain were married 22nd March, 1752—(their children):

47. (1) James Shine, the son of John Shine and Sarah, his wife, was born the 30th day of January—i.e., the year of our Lord, 1753.
48. (2) Elizabeth Shine was born the 6th of August, 1754.
49. (3) Eleanor Shine was born the 24th of September, 1756.
50. (4) John Shine was born the 22nd of November, 1758.
51. (5) Francis Shine was born the 24th of March, 1761.
52. (6) Hannah Shine was born the 18th of June, 1762.
53. (7) Mary Shine was born the 7th of June, 1765.
54. (8) Elizabeth Shine was born the 7th of June, 1765.
55. (9) William Shine was born the 26th of September, 1768.
56. (10) Daniel Shine was born the 3rd of July, 1771.
57. (11) Nancy Shine was born the 14th of October, 1772.
        The ages of John Shine's children deceased, December the 12th, 1783.

In the year 1790, there were several families of the name Shine in North Carolina. The United States census, taken in that year, gives the following entries of the heads of families:

NORTH CAROLINA.

Halifax District—Halifax County.

58. Shine, James—
     Free white males of 16 years and upwards, including heads of families   2

Free white males under 16 years   2
Free white females, including heads of families   6
Slaves   1

Randolph County.

59. Shine, Jacob—
Free white males of 16 years and upwards, including heads of families   3
Free white males under 16 years   1
Free white females, including heads of families   6

Craven County.

60. Shine, William—
Free white males of 16 years and upwards including heads of families   1
Free white males under 16 years   2
Free white females, including heads of families   3
Slaves   8

Dobbs County.

61. Shine, Francis—
Free white males of 16 years and upwards, including heads of families   1
Free white females, including heads of families   4
Slaves   1

Jones County.

62. Shine, John—
Free white males of 16 years and upwards, including heads of families   1
Free white males under 16 years   3
Free white females, including heads of families   5
Slaves   8

63. Shine, Daniel—
Free white males of 16 years and upwards, including heads of
families   3
Free white females, including heads of families   3
Slaves   12

MARYLAND.

Frederick County.

64. Shine, Philip—
Free white males of 16 years and upwards, including heads of
families   3
Free white males under 16 years   2
Free white females, including heads of families   4

The settlement in North Carolina appears to be in different counties of the state and in some instances some distance apart. Halifax County is in the north central; Randolph County about central; Craven County and Jones County are in the southeastern part of State; Dobbs County is in the southeastern part of the state.

The families mentioned in the United States census of 1790 are no doubt descendants of the one or more of the three brothers who came from Dublin. As the family names were much the same it is difficult to determine the exact relationship of various members of the several families.

This Daniel Shine who married Elizabeth Greene, May 15, 1715, was one of the three brothers who came from Dublin. He settled in New Bern District, North Carolina. Francis Shine, one of the other brothers, settled in Duplin County, N. C., and the other brother, James or John, settled in Virginia. This is the family tradition and in all probability substantially correct. We have no data as to the name of the father of the three brothers who immigrated to America in those early days. However, as it was customary in Ireland to name the oldest son after the grandfather, we may assume that his name was John. Daniel's oldest son we find was named John, and no doubt was named after the grandfather following the prevailing custom of the times. Whether the family resided at Dublin, or the brothers only sailed from that city, is a matter

43

of conjecture. However, inasmuch as the Shines for centuries were settled in the Counties of Cork, Limerick and Kerry, this family in all probability came from some one of these counties. We designate these as the first of the family to settle in America, as we have been unable to trace from the John Shine who is referred to in the Massachusetts records.

FIRST GENERATION IN AMERICA.

Daniel Shine (1). Francis Shine (1). James or John Shine (1).

33. **Major Daniel Shine** (1) married Elizabeth Greene, May 15, 1715. He came from Dublin, Ireland, about the year 1710. He settled at New Bern, N. C., and in all probability married there. He was a major in the army. There were many families of Greene in the colonies as early as 1790, when the U. S. census was taken, and it is evident from the number at that time that there were many families of that name there in the early part of the 18th century.

Their children were:

65.	(1)	Hannah Shine, born July 16, 1718.
66.	(2)	Elizabeth Shine, born February 19, 1721.
67.	(3)	Mary Shine, born July 11, 1724.
68.	(4)	John Shine, born Nov. 25, 1725.
69.	(5)	Mary Shine, born Dec. 27, 1727.
70.	(6)	Daniel Shine, born May 10, 1729.
71.	(7)	James Shine, born Jan. 9, 1731.
72.	(8)	Sarah Shine, born Feby. 7, 1732.
73.	(9)	Thomas Shine, born Oct. 1, 1736.
74.	(10)	Francis Shine, born June 25th, 1741.

We have been unable to learn anything definite regarding any of the children of Daniel Shine (1) and Elizabeth Green, excepting their son, John Shine, and his descendants.

(2) **Francis Shine** (1), one of the three brothers who came from Dublin about 1710. He settled in Duplin County, N. C. We have been unable to get definite information as to his posterity.

44

(3) **James** or **John Shine** (1). It is said he settled in Virginia, but we are without further data as for this or his descendants.

SECOND GENERATION.

68. John Shine (2). Daniel Shine (1).

John Shine; fourth child of Daniel Shine and Elizabeth Greene, was born Nov. 25th, 1725, presumably in New Bern, N. C. He married Sarah Shelweain, March 22nd, 1752. Their children were:

75.	(1)	James Shine, born Jan. 30th, 1753.
76.	(2)	Elizabeth Shine, born Aug. 6th, 1754.
77.	(3)	Eleanor Shine, born Sept. 24th, 1756.
78.	(4)	John Shine, born Nov. 22nd, 1758.
79.	(5)	Francis Shine, born March 24th, 1761.
80.	(6)	Hannah Shine, born June 18th, 1763.
81.	(7)	Elizabeth Shine, born June 7th, 1765.
82.	(8)	William Shine, born Sept. 26th, 1768.
83.	(9)	Daniel Shine, born July 3rd, 1771.
84.	(10)	Nancy Shine, born Oct. 14th, 1772.

70. Daniel Shine (2). Daniel Shine (1).

Colonel Daniel Shine, sixth son of Daniel Shine and Elizabeth Greene, was born May 10th, 1729. He married Barbara Franck, and lived in Jones County, N. C. In his will, made April 6, 1801, and probated in May, 1801, seven children are mentioned, viz.:

85.	(1)	Polly Shine Shackleford.
86.	(2)	John Shine.
87.	(3)	Susanna Shine Wilton.
88.	(4)	Hannah Shine Farnal.
89.	(5)	Daniel Shine.
90.	(6)	Col. James Shine.
91.	(7)	Franck Shine.

Colonel Daniel Shine was a colonel in the army of the ——. His wife, Barbara Franck was of a very distinguished family. She lived to a very old age. They were great friends of George Washington. Mention of Mrs. Shine is made in the book entitled, "Our Living and Our Dead," in the state library at Raleigh, N. C., as follows:

> "Colonel Daniel Shine's widow (Barbara Franck), of Cypress Creek, N. C., lived to the great age of 95 years. She entertained George Washington when he made his famous southern trip."

In the will of Colonel Daniel Shine, probated in 1801, he refers to some of his estate as:

> "200 acres called the 'Royal Oak,'"

and another

> "200 acres of land, patented by myself, lying on the head of Big Cypress Creek."

72. Sarah Shine (2). Daniel (1).

Sarah Shine, the eighth child of Daniel Shine and Elizabeth Greene, born February 7th, 1732, married a Mr. Kenass or Kinast, and settled in Duplin County, N. C.

THIRD GENERATION.

75. James Shine (3). John Shine (2). Daniel Shine (1).

James Shine, the first child of John Shine and Sarah Shelweain, was born January 30th, 1753, in New Berne, N. C. We have been unable to learn anything more of him.

81. Elizabeth Shine (3). John Shine (2). Daniel Shine (1).

Elizabeth Shine.—There appears to have been two of that name in the family, one born Aug. 6th, 1754, and the other, June 7th, 1765. After careful consideration, with such data as I have at hand, I have concluded that this John Shine who married Sarah Shelweain, married a second time, and that his second wife's name was Eleanor McIver, and that of the children of this latter marriage was Elizabeth Shine, No. 7, in the enumeration of children of this John Shine.

ADMIRAL FARRAGUT
(Seated)

This Elizabeth Shine, I take it, was the mother of Admiral David Glasgow Farragut. In the life of Admiral Farragut, by his son, Loyall Farragut, it is stated that Major Farragut married Elizabeth Shine, born in 1765, and a daughter of John Shine and Eleanor McIver of Dobbs County, N. C. And in memorandum notes of Loyall Farragut the names of two of the children of John Shine and Eleanor McIver are given, and they are Elizabeth Shine, born in Dobbs County, 1765, married 1796, to Major George Farragut, and Nancy Shine, married June 5th, 1804, to Archibald Trimble. Now the youngest of the family of John Shine was named Nancy, and the date of her birth, Oct. 14th, 1772; she would be thirty-two years old at the date of her marriage. Her sister, Elizabeth, was 31. Newbern was near Dobbs County, and no doubt the main postoffice at that time. They are, in my opinion, the same persons mentioned in the Farragut pedigree. However, this is subject to further consideration.

77. Eleanor Shine (3). John Shine (2). Daniel Shine (1).

Eleanor Shine, the third child of John Shine and Sarah Shelweain, was born Sept. 24th, 1756. She married a Mr. Chestnut and settled in Duplin County, N.C.

Mr. J. Walter R. Bozeman, of Atlanta, Georgia, a son of Virginia Harrison Shine, a daughter of James Bryan Shine, and granddaughter of Colonel James Shine and Leah Yates, having given the family history some study, is of the opinion that Daniel Shine, who married Elizabeth Greene, was a nephew of Major Daniel Shine, whose will was probated May 9th, 1857. It is true that the names of his children, mentioned in the will are not exactly the same as the names of the children of Daniel Shine and Elizabeth Greene, but so far as they are mentioned they are the same, except that in the will there is a William, while in the other there is a Francis, and as the same person may have both names, this difference would not be conclusive against it being the same person. However, I give the following genealogical tabulation of Mr. Bozeman:

GENEALOGICAL RECORD OF THE SHINE FAMILY
(BY J. W. R. BOZEMAN.)

Maj. Daniel Shine, of Craven County, North Carolina. Will probated (no record of wife) May 9th, 1757. The following are his children as mentioned in said will:

John,

Thomas,

Williams,

Elizabeth Vaughn,

James.

It seems probable that the above Maj. Daniel Shine is an uncle of the following descendant:

Daniel Shine—married Elizabeth Greene May 15th, 1715; their children were:

(1)   Hannah Shine, born July 16, 1718.
(2)   Elizabeth Shine, born Feby. 19, 1721.
(3)   Mary Shine, born July 11, 1724.
(4)   John Shine, born Nov. 25, 1725.
(5)   Mary Shine, born Dec. 27, 1727.
(6)   Daniel Shine, born May 10, 1729.
(7)   James Shine, born Jan. 9, 1731.
(8)   Sarah Shine, born Feby. 7, 1732.
(9)   Thomas Shine, born Oct. 1, 1736.
(10)   Francis Shine, born June 25, 1741.

John Shine (No. 4) a son of Daniel Shine and Elizabeth Green, married Sarah Shelweain March 22nd, 1752. Their children were:

(1)   James Shine, born Jan. 30, 1753.
(2)   Elizabeth Shine, born Aug. 6, 1754.
(3)   Eleanor Shine, born Sept. 24, 1756.
(4)   John Shine, born Nov. 22, 1758.
(5)   Francis Shine, born March 24, 1761.
(6)   Hannah Shine, born June 18, 1763.

(7)   Elizabeth Shine, born June 7, 1765.
(8)   William Shine, born Sept. 26, 1768.
(9)   Daniel Shine, born July 3, 1771.
(10)   Nancy Shine, born Oct. 14, 1772.

Capt. Daniel Shine, J. P. (No. 6) son of Daniel Shine and Elizabeth Greene, born May 10, 1729, married Barbara Franck (daughter of John Martin Franck). Will probated in court, May term, 1801, Jones County, N. C. The following are their children, as mentioned in said will:

(1)   Polly Shackelford,
(2)   John,
(3)   Susanna Wilton,
(4)   Hannah Farnal,
(5)   Daniel,
(6)   James,
(7)   Franck.

Col. James Shine (No. 6), son of Daniel Shine and Barbara Franck, married Leah Yates. Served in "Revolution;" paid off at Halifax, N. C., 1784 and 1785. Also served in North Carolina Legislature, 1815 and 1816. Their children were:

(1)   Daniel Y.
(2)   James Bryan.
(3)   Hannah A., and others that cannot be recorded at this date.

James Bryan Shine (No. 2), son of Col. James Shine and Leah Yates, of New Bern, N. C., Jones County, married Miss Rebecca Harrison, Nov. 19th, 1831. Their children were:

(1)   Ann.
(2)   Hannah A.
(3)   Daniel Y.
(4)   Simmons.
(5)   Elizabeth.
(6)   James.
(7)   Virginia Harrison Shine (my mother).

79. Francis Shine, also called Francis Stringer Shine (3). John Shine (2). Daniel Shine (1).

Francis Stringer Shine, fifth child of John Shine and Sarah (Shelweian) Shine, was born March 24th, 1761, at New Bern, Craven County, N. C., but afterwards lived in Sampson County, N. C. He married Agnes Ann Torrence, Feb. 7, 1795; their children were:

92.	(1)	James Shine.
93.	(2)	John Shine, born June 2, 1804; m. Martha Rhodes.
94.	(3)	William Shine.
95.	(4)	Margaret Shine; married Judge John Killen and settled in ———.
96.	(5)	Richard Alexander Shine, b. June 23, 1812; m. Mary Ann Maultsby.
97.	(6)	Thomas Torrence Shine, m.
98.	(7)	Ellen Shine (Rawls).
99.	(8)	Sarah Shine (Peacock).

Thomas Torrence, Ellen and Sarah are not given by some in describing the family, and by others are given as above.

90. Colonel James Shine (3). Daniel Shine (2). Daniel Shine (1).

Colonel James Shine, the sixth child of Colonel Daniel Shine and Barbara Franck, was born in Jones County, N. C. He married Leah Yates. Their children were:

100.	(1)	James Bryan Shine; m. Rebecca Harrison, Mar. 19, 1831.
101.	(2)	Daniel Yates Shine.
102.	(3)	Hannah A, Shine; m. Frederick J. Jones.

Colonel James Shine served in the Revolutionary war; was paid off at Halifax, N. C., 1784-1785. He served in the North Carolina Legislature, 1815-1816.

93. John Shine (4). Francis Stringer Shine (3). John Shine (2). Daniel Shine (1).

John Shine, the second child of Francis Stringer Shine and Agnes Ann Torrence, born June 2nd, 1804, died Nov. 8th, 1881. He was born at New Berne, and married Martha Rhodes in 1826. They had thirteen children, ten of whom grew to man and womanhood. They were:

103.	(1)	Mary Farrior Shine.
104.	(2)	James Francis Shine, born in 1830; living in 1910.
105.	(3)	Joseph Alexander Shine
106.	(4)	Margaret Ann Shine, born 1834; m. a Mr. Herring; living in 1910.
107.	(5)	John Daniel Shine.
108.	(6)	Thomas William Shine.
109.	(7)	Louisa Marion Shine; born, 1840; died, 1858.
110.	(8)	Carolina Virginia Shine.
111.	(9)	Sarah Eleanor Shine; died at 18 years.
112.	(10)	Junius Augustus Shine; born May 10, 1851.

96. Richard Alexander Shine (4). Francis Stinger Shine (3). John Shine (2). Daniel Shine (1).

Richard Alexander Shine, the fourth child of Francis Stringer Shine and Agnes Ann Torrence, was born June 23rd, 1812, and married Mary Ann Maultsby, of Fayetteville, N. C., Sept. 27th, 1832. They came, as bride and groom, to Tallahasse, Fla., where they settled in 1835. Their children were:

113.	(1)	James Miller Shine; m. Sallie Grice.
114.	(2)	Richard Alexander Shine; m. Laura Fisher.
115.	(3)	William Francis Shine; m. Maria Jefferson Eppes.
116.	(4)	John Shine (died young).
117.	(5)	Thomas Jabez Shine; m. Martha Virginia Eppes.
118.	(6)	Henry Rutgers Shine; m. Amanda Robertson.

119. (7)   Lillian Eleanor Shine (died single).
120. (8)   Mary Kate Shine (died single).
121. (9)   Laura Shine (died single).
122. (10) Warton Hume Shine; m. Mary Amelia Gates.
123. (11) David Shepard Shine; m. Carolina Matilda Eppes.
124. (12) Elizabeth Agnes Shine; m. Richard Starkey, second husband, Seth Woodruff.

102. Hannah A. Shine (4). James Shine (3). Daniel Shine (2). Daniel Shine (1).

Hannah A. Shine, the third child of James Shine and Leah Yates, born in Jones County, N. C., in 1810. She married Frederick J. Jones. Their children were:

125. (1)   Leah Myra Jones, born Sept. 29, 1834; m. George Allen; d. Oct. 22, 1910.
126. (2)   Mary Eliza Jones; born Sept. 30, 1836; m. L. C. Vass; settled at Schenectady, N. Y.
127. (3)   Daniel Shine Jones; born 1845; m. Leah B. Holland, 1889.
128. (4)   Eleanor Stratton Jones; born Sept. 24, 1851; m. George N. Ives, of New Berne, N. C. No children.

100. James Bryan Shine (4). Colonel James Shine (3). Colonel Daniel Shine (2). Major Daniel Shine (1).

James Bryan Shine, the second child of Colonel James Shine and Leah Yates, was born in the year ——, at ——. He married Rebecca Harrison, Nov. 19, 1831, and settled at New Bern, Jones County, N. C. Their children were:

129. (1)   Ann Shine.
130. (2)   Hannah A. Shine.
131. (3)   Daniel Y. Shine.
132. (4)   Simmons Shine.
133. (5)   Elizabeth Shine.
134. (6)   James Shine.
135. (7)   Virginia Harrison Shine.

FIFTH GENERATION.

114. Richard Alexander Shine (5). Richard A. Shine (4). Francis Stringer Shine (3). John Shine (2). Daniel Shine (1).

Richard Alexander Shine, the second child of Richard A. Shine and Mary Ann Maultsby, was born at Tallahassee, in the year ——. He married Laura Fisher and resided at Tallahassee, Fla. Their children were:

136.	(1)	John Harvard Shine (now deceased).
137.	(2)	Leila Shine; m. James G. Beggs.
138.	(3)	Mary Shine (now deceased).
139.	(4)	Laura Shine (now deceased).
140.	(5)	Richard A. Shine; m. Pauline Brooks.
141.	(6)	Henry Rutgers Shine (now deceased).
142.	(7)	Nell Shine (now deceased).
143.	(8)	Cheever Lewis Shine, single.
144.	(9)	Hugh Shine (now deceased).
145.	(10)	Albert Shine, single.

113. James Miller Shine (5). Richard A. Shine (4). Francis Stringer Shine (3). John Shine (2). Daniel Shine (1).

James Miller Shine, the first child of Richard A. Shine and Mary Maultsby, was born ——, at Tallahassee, Fla. He married Sallie Grice, at ——, in the year ——. Their children were:

146.	(1)	Richard Keenan Shine (now deceased).
147.	(2)	Walter Newton Shine.
148.	(3)	Charles Francis Shine.
149.	(4)	Clarence James Miller Shine.

115. William Francis Shine (5). Richard A. Shine (4). Francis Stringer Shine (3). John Shine (2). Daniel Shine (1).

William Francis Shine, the third child of Richard A. Shine and Mary Ann Maultsby, was born at Tallahassee, Fla., in the year ——. He married Maria

Jefferson Eppes, a great granddaughter of President Thomas Jefferson, and settled at St. Augustine. Their children were:

150.   Francis Eppes Shine, born Jan. 13, 1871.

122. Wharton Hume Shine (5). Richard A. Shine (4). Francis Stringer Shine (3). John Shine (2). Daniel Shine (1).

Wharton Hume Shine, the tenth child of Richard A. Shine and Mary Ann Maultsby, married Amelia Gates; they had no children.

117. Thomas Jabez Shine (5). Richard A. Shine (4). Francis Stringer Shine (3). John Shine (2). Daniel Shine (1).

Thomas Jabez Shine, the fifth child of Richard A. Shine and Mary Ann Maultsby, was born at Tallahassee, in the year ——. He married Martha Virginia Eppes, a great granddaughter of Thomas Jefferson, ex-President of the United States in 1866; died in 1889. Their children were:

151. (1)   Lillian Eleanor Shine; b. Madison, Fla.
152. (2)   Francis Wayles Shine; b. Orlando, Fla.
153. (3)   Richard Alexander Shine; b. Orlando, Fla.
154. (4)   William Eston Eppes Shine; b. Orlando, Fla.

123. David Sheperd Shine (5). Richard A. Shine (4). Francis Stringer Shine (3). John Shine (2). Daniel Shine (1).

David Sheperd Shine, the eleventh child of Richard A. Shine and Mary Ann Maultsby, was born at Tallahassee, in the year ——. He married Caroline Matilda Eppes, a great granddaughter of Thomas Jefferson, the third President of the United States, Oct. 31st, 1882, and settled at Orlando, Fla. Their children were:

155. (1)   Dudley Sheperd Shine; m. Theodocia Morison, Dec. 29,
                  1909.
156. (2)   Wharton Hume Shine (deceased).
157. (3)   Cecil Eppes Shine (single).

158. (4) Margaret Virginia Shine (single).
159. (5) Lillian Agnes Shine (now deceased).

118. Henry Rutgers Shine (5). Richard A. Shine (4). Francis Stringer Shine (3). John Shine (2). Daniel Shine (1).

Henry Rutgers Shine, the sixth child of Richard A. Shine and Mary Ann Maultsby, was born at ——, in the year ——. He married Amanda Robertson. Their children were:

160. (1) Amanda Shine (single).
161. (2) Mary Shine (single).
162. (3) Thomas Shine.
163. (4) Belle Shine.
164. (5) Lillie Shine (single).
165. (6) Florida Shine (single).
166. (7) William Shine; m. Mary Gates.
167. (8) Henry Shine.
169. (9) Eloise Shine.
170. (10) Mildred Shine (single).
171. (11) Lala Shine (single).

103. Mary Farrior Shine (5). John Shine (4). Francis Stringer Shine (3). John Shine (2). Daniel Shine (1).

Mary Farrior Shine, the first child of John Shine and Martha Rhodes, was born at ——, in the year ——. She married I. B. Kelley, in the year 1864, and settled at Kenensville, N. C. Their children were:

172. Martha Rhodes Kelly.

104. James Francis Shine (5). John Shine (4). Francis Stringer Shine (3). John Shine (2). Daniel Shine (1).

James Francis Shine, the second child of John Shine and Martha Rhodes, was born at ——, in the year 1830. He married—first wife, Clara Hodges;

second wife, Elizabeth Nixon; third wife, Eliza Hodges. Their children (but by which wife is unknown) were:

173. (1)   Walter N. Shine.
174. (2)   Arthur J. Shine.
175. (3)   Clara H. Shine.
176. (4)   Lee J. Shine.
177. (5)   John D. Shine.

105. Joseph Alexander Shine (5). John Shine (4). Francis Stringer Shine (3). John Shine (2). Daniel Shine (1).

Joseph Alexander Shine, the third child of John Shine and Martha Rhodes, was born at ——, in the year —— .He married Carrie C. Blaunt, in 1857, and resided at Mt. Olive, N. C. Their children were:

178.   John Edgar Shine—not living in 1910.

106. Margaret Ann Shine (5). John Shine (4). Francis Stringer Shine (3). John Shine (2). Daniel Shine (1).

Margaret Ann Shine, the fourth child of John Shine and Martha Rhodes, was born at ——, in the year ——. She married N. W. Herring, M. D., in the year 1860, and resided at Kenensville, N. C. Their children were:

179. (1)   Julia P. Herring.
180. (2)   John Shine Herring.
181. (3)   George W. Herring.
182. (4)   Pattee R. Herring.
183. (5)   James Alexander Herring.

107. John Daniel Shine (5). John Shine (4). Francis Stringer Shine (3). John Shine (2). Daniel Shine (1).

John Daniel Shine, the fifth child of John Shine and Martha Rhodes, was born at ——, in the year ——. He never married. He fought in the Civil war; was color bearer in Company E, Regiment 20, North Carolina troops. He was mortally wounded at the battle of Cald Narbaus, in Virginia. He won high honors for his bravery in battle.

108. Thomas William Shine (5). John Shine (4). Francis Stringer Shine (3). John Shine (2). Daniel Shine (1).

Thomas William Shine, the sixth child of John Shine and Martha Rhodes, was born at ——, in the year ——. He married Emma Kirkwood, in the, year 1882, and settled at Orlando, Fla. They had one child, not living in 1910.

110. Carolina Virginia Shine (5). John Shine (4). Francis Stringer Shine (3) John Shine (2). Daniel Shine (1).

Carolina Virginia Shine, the eighth child of John Shine and Martha Rhodes, was born at ——, in the year ——. She married Nathan J. King in the year 1870, and settled in Sampson County, N. C. Their children were:

184.	(1)	Mary Rhodes King.
185.	(2)	Carrie Law King.
186.	(3)	Junius A. King.
187.	(4)	James A. King.
188.	(5)	Julia King.

112. Junius Augustus Shine (5). John Shine (4). Francis Stringer Shine (3). John Shine (2). Daniel Shine (1).

Junius Augustus Shine, the tenth child of John Shine and Martha Rhodes, was born at Faison, Duplin County, N. C., May 10, 1851. He married Salle Elizabeth Bawden, in the year 1882, and settled on the farm where he was born, at Faison. Their children were:

189.	(1)	Henry Bawden Shine.
190.	(2)	Thomas William Shine.
191.	(3)	Pattie Rhodes Shine.
192.	(4)	Daniel Bawden Shine.
193.	(5)	John Faison Shine.
194.	(6)	Edna Ann Shine.

195. (7) Margaret Pake Shine.
196. (8) Junius Augustus Shine, Jr.

127. Daniel Shine Jones (5). Hannah A. Shine (4). James Shine (3). Daniel Shine (2). Daniel Shine (1).

Daniel Shine Jones, the third child of Frederick J. Jones and Hannah A. Shine, was born at New Berne, N. C., in the year 1845. He married Leah B. Holland, in the year 1889, and settled at New Berne, N. C. Their children were:

197.   Frederick J. Jones, born in 1890.

Daniel Shine Jones served through the Civil war, in the 10th N. C. Infantry.

125. Leah Myra Jones (5). Hannah A. Shine (4). James Shine (3). Daniel Shine (2). Daniel Shine (1).

Leah Myra Jones, daughter of Hannah A. Shine and Frederick J. Jones, was born at New Bern, N. C., Sept. 29, 1834, and died Oct. 22, 1910. She married George Allen and settled at ——. Their children were:

198. (1)   Mary Hannah Allen, born Apr., 1862; died June, 1862.
199. (2)   Hannah Shine Allen, born May, 1863 (Mrs. Charles S. Ises), New Bern.
200. (3)   Eliza Slover Allen, born Oct., 1865; died Dec., 1876.
201. (4)   Mary Louise Allen, born Nov., 1866 (Mrs. Wm. H. Porter), Boston.
202. (5)   Susan Lucretia Allen, born Jan., 1868; died Dec. 1876.
203. (6)   Myra Vass Allen, born July, 1869; died June, 1870.
204. (7)   Leah Jones Allen, born May, 1870; died June, 1871.
205. (8)   George Cushing Allen, born Jan., 1872; died June 1872.
206. (9)   Frederick Jones Allen, born Feb., 1873; died Dec., 1876.
207. (10) George Edward Allen, born Aug, 1874; died Dec., 1876.
208. (11) Charles John Allen, born Oct., 1875; died Nov., 1876.
209. (12) Harry Vass Allen, born Dec., 1877; living in New York.
           (Five of these children died of dyptheria within two weeks—Nov.-Dec., 1876.)

126. Mary Eliza Jones (5). Hannah A. Shine (4). James Shine (3). Daniel Shine (2). Daniel Shine (1).

Mary Eliza Jones, daughter of Hannah A. Shine and Frederick J. Jones, was born at New Bern, N. C., Sept. 30, 1836. She married L. C. Vass and settled at Schenectady, N. Y. Their children were:

210. (1)   Leah Allen Vass, born March 27, 1869.
211. (2)   Elizabeth Maury Vass, born May 24, 1870.
212. (3)   Lanchlan Cumming Vass, born Feb. 22, 1872.
213. (4)   Eleanor Shine Vass, born July 24, 1873.
214. (5)   Edward Smallwood Vass, born Feb. 23, 1875.

150. Francis Eppes Shine (6). William Francis Shine (5). Richard A. Shine (4). Francis Stringer Shine (3). John Shine (2). Daniel Shine (1).

Dr. Francis Eppes Shine, the only child of William Francis Shine and Maria Jefferson Eppes, was born at St. Augustine, Fla., Jan. 13th, 1871. He married Annie Barker, of Toronto, Ont., in the year 1904, and settled at Bisbee, Arizona. Their children were:

215. (1)   Francis Eppes Shine, Jr., born May 13, 1905.
216. (2)   Randolph Eppes Shine, born July 1st, 1906.
217. (3)   Elizabeth Shine, born Nov. 7, 1911.

He graduated from the University of the South at Sewanee, Tenn., in 1892; after leaving Sewanee, he entered the University of Virginia and graduated from the Medical Department in the year 1895. He then entered the New York Hospital as interne, in 1896, and graduated from that hospital in 1899. He settled in New York City and engaged in the practice of his profession. His ability was soon recognized, and in 1901 he was appointed as instructor in G. U. Surgery, Cornell University, medical department (City of New York). On account of his health, however, he was obliged to leave New York, and in 1903, accepted the appointment as Chief Surgeon for the Copper Queen Consolidated Mining Company and the El Paso Southwestern Railroad, and moved to Bisbee, Arizona, where he was residing in 1911, engaged in the practice of his profession.

153. Richard Alexander Shine (6). Thomas Jabez Shine (5). Richard A. Shine (4). Francis Stringer Shine (3). John Shine (2). Daniel Shine (1).

Richard Alexander Shine, the third child of Thomas Jabez Shine and Martha Virginia Eppes, was born at ——, in the year 18——; married Rosebud Boyd. He settled at Miami, Fla., where he was, in 1912, engaged in the insurance business.

152. Francis Wayles Shine (6). Thomas Jabez Shine (5). Richard A. Shine (4). Francis Stringer Shine (3). John Shine (2). Daniel Shine (1).

Francis Wayles Shine, the second child of Thomas Jabez Shine and Martha Virginia Eppes, was born at ——, in the year 18——; married ——. He took up the medical profession, and in 1909 was practicing his profession in New York City.

154. William Eston Eppes Shine (6). Thomas Jabez Shine (5). Richard A. Shine (4). Francis Stringer Shine (3). John Shine (2). Daniel Shine (1).

William Eston Eppes Shine, the fourth child of Thomas Jabez Shine and Martha Virginia Eppes, was born at ——, in the year 1878. He received his preliminary education in the high school at ——, and graduated from the —— law department in 1899. He located at Orlando, Fla., and engaged in the practice of his profession. He married Florence Dunn Howard, April 19, 1911. He rose rapidly in his profession and was regarded as one of the most promising members of the bar. He died suddenly, at New York City, January 8, 1913, and was buried at Orlando, Fla.

CHAPTER VII.

SHINE FAMILY IN THE STATE OF NEW YORK.

218. Thomas Joseph Shine (1).

Thomas Joseph Shine, now (1913) residing at 50 Clinton Place, New York City, was born in the month of August, 1839, at Charleville, Ireland. He was a son of Dennis Shine and Honora Power (see records of baptism for the records of the church at Charleville). He had three brothers, Patrick, John and William, and four sisters, Catherine, Eliza, Kate and Mary. Charleville lies close to the county line, between the counties Cork and Limerick, and is about the center of the district in which the Shines lived, and no doubt that is a branch of the same family.

Thomas Joseph Shine left Charleville about the year 1864 and located in New York City. He married Catherine M. Kelly at New York, June 13th, 1869; he engaged in business in New York, and after many years of successful business life, retired from business in 1909. Their children were:

219. (1) William P. J. Shine, born Oct. 14, 1870; m. Elizabeth J. Murphy, Nov. 30, 1905.
220. (2) Thomas F. Shine, born March 1, 1874.
221. (3) Annie G. Shine, born Nov. 29, 1876; m. Wm. J. Goff, July 11, 1912.
222. (4) Bernard J. Shine, born Feb. 15, 1882.
223. (5) Edward J. Shine, born Jan. 1st, 1885.
224. (6) James R. Shine, born Feb. 10, 1887.

A family of Shine also resided at Tonawanda, N. Y., and is said to be related to the branch living in New York City.

There was also living (1911) in Troy, N. Y., a family Shyne.

REV. PATRICK SHINE.

CHAPTER VIII.

THE SHINE FAMILY IN OHIO.

225. **Jerome Shine** and family settled at Sidney, Ohio, in 1850. This is the first settlement of the Shine family in Ohio, so far as I have been able to discover. Jerome Shine came from New Market, County Cork, Ireland. His father, Jerome Shine, Sr., was born at Freemont, County Cork, Ireland, and settled at New Market. He had three brothers and two sisters, Bartholomew, William, Eugene, Mary and Julia, which were uncles and aunts of Jerome Shine who emigrated to Sidney, Ohio. We have no information of the brothers and sisters of Jerome Shine, Sr., except that his brother, Bartholomew Shine, never married, and one of the sons of either William or Eugene Shine was a priest at Killarney for over sixty years. His name was Patrick Shine.

He died about 1893, and was over eighty years of age at the time of his death. Jerome Shine was born at New Market, in 1779. He was married twice, but we are unable to give the name of either wife. However, the children by his first wife were:

226.	(1)	Bartholomew Shine, born May 2, 1828.
227.	(2)	Daniel Shine—was in Civil war, never returned.
228.	(3)	Ellen Shine; m. P. M. Bowler.
229.	(4)	Johana Shine; m. Lem Compton. By his second wife.
230.	(5)	William Shine, born 1842.
231.	(6)	Annie Shine.
232.	(7)	Dennis Shine.
233.	(8)	Jerome Shine.

All but the youngest of the family were born in Ireland. The family came to Sidney, Ohio, about the year 1850. Shortly after settling at Sidney, a relative, named Michael Shine, lived with them for sometime. It is thought that Michael J. Shine, of Toledo, Ohio, was a son of his. Michael J. Shine was a prominent member of the Knights of Columbus. Jerome Shine died at Sidney, Ohio, in April, 1856, at the age of 77 years.

SECOND GENERATION.

226. Bartholomew Shine (2). Jerome Shine (1).

Bartholomew Shine, the first child of Jerome Shine and —— Shine, was born at New Market, County Cork, Ireland, May 2, 1828. He came to Sidney, Ohio, with his parents in 1850. He was named after his grand uncle, Bartholomew Shine, priest at Bresna, Co. Kerry, who died about the year 1828, at the age of 80 years. Bartholomew Shine married in 1853 and resided at Cleveland, Ohio, in 1903. Their children were:

BARTHOLOMEW SHINE.

234. (1)   William Shine.
235. (2)   Jerome Shine.
236. (3)   Julia Shine.
237. (4)   Maggie Shine.
238. (5)   Mary Shine.

Bartholomew Shine was a man of fine physique; was six feet and two inches in heighth, and weighed 235 pounds, and of the healthy rugged type. He followed railroad contracting and built many miles of railroad in the State of Ohio.

229. Johana Shine (2). Jerome Shine (1).

Johana Shine, the youngest child of Jerome Shine and ——, was born in the year 18——, at New Market, County Cork, Ireland. She came with her parents to Sidney, Ohio, about the year 1850. She married Lem Compton, in the year 18——, and resided at Peavine, Nevada. Died about the year 1901. Their children are:

The following is a reproduction of a letter to Mr. Lem Compton, written by one T. E. Shine, in 1886:

"Silverada, White Pine Co., Nevada, Dec. 5, 1886.

Mr. Lem Compton, Belmont.

Sir: Through the courtesy of Mr. James A. Logan, who paid us a visit a few days ago, I received some information of a namesake of mine who I understand is your wife, and as the name is so scarce in this country, Mr. Logan requested me to drop you and her respectively a few lines. Mr. Logan's information to me is to the effect that your wife is a native of the south of Ireland, as so is mine. My parents immigrated to America in the year 1825 or '26, and settled in the State of Connecticut, where they raised a family of seven children, five girls and two boys, your humble servant being one who, as you are aware, immigrated to the Pacific coast very young, been to a great many of the old excitements through Nevada, White Pine among the balance, where I remember Lem Compton working in the Spring of '69, together with Bill Fought and some more of the boys. Lem, there has been a great many changes made since then, for instance, look at our old friend, 'Jim' Logan, and see what he has gone through—that man went through enough to kill a dozen men to my knowledge.

LEM COMPTON.
JOHANA SHINE COMPTON.

Now, in regard to your wife, there may be some relationship existing between her and I as there was a large family of the Shines that never immigrated to this country and who still reside in Ireland. I believe their native country is Cork or Limerick, somewhere close to the line of both counties. At the death of my grandfather, my mother paid that country a visit with the intention of receiving some dowery which was stipulated in the will. I believe her amount was $1,000 or something like that, but it makes no difference, she never received a cent. It seemed that the Irish gladiators were too much for the old woman, and as the saying is; she got left.

Now, in conclusion, I would say that I would be very happy to receive a few lines from you and your respective wife, and as I have lots of leisure time evenings, we may trace up some relationship; whether or not the name is sufficient to have a kindly feeling towards each other. I will bring my letter to a close by sending my best wishes to you and your wife. I remain,

Respectfully your humble friend,

T. E. Shine."

228. Ellen Shine (2). Jerome Shine (1).

ELLEN SHINE.

Ellen Shine, the second child of Jerome Shine and ——, was born at New Market, County Cork, Ireland, about the year 1830. She came with the family to Sidney, Ohio, about the year 1850. She married P. M. Bowler in the year 18——, and settled at ——. She was living in 1905. Their children are:

230. William Shine (2). Jerome Shine (1).

William Shine, the fifth child of Jerome Shine and first child of his second marriage, was born at New Market, County Cork, Ireland, about the year 1842. He, with his father's family, came to Sidney, Ohio, about the year 1850. He continued to reside at Sidney. He married ——, about the year 18——, and raised a family of three boys (all young men m 1905):

239. (1)   John B. Shine.
240. (2)   —— Shine.
241. (3)   —— Shine.

William Shine became a successful and leading man at Sidney. He took a prominent part in politics and was regarded as one of the strong men in the State of Ohio. The following personal reference was clipped from one of the leading papers of that state:

"William Shine, of this city, has been selected as a member of the State Democratic Executive Committee, by the State Democratic Central Committee, receiving the unanimous vote of the Central Committee. Mr. Shine has been a great worker in the Democratic party for many years and is thoroughly posted on the politics of Ohio. He is also widely known among the workers of the party over the State and is regarded by them as one of the best organizers in the party. His selection was made at the request of candidates on the State ticket. His ability, wide acquaintance and knowledge, of politics will make him a valuable member on the committee."

There were also two families of Shine residing in Toledo, Ohio, in 1905. Michael J. Shine, 708 Summitt Street, and Thomas Shine, 317 Western Ave. It is said they are brothers and sons of the Michael Shine who visited for a while with the Shines of Sidney, Ohio, and supposed to be related to them.

WILLIAM SHINE.

CHAPTER IX.

THE SHINE FAMILY IN WASHINGTON.

242. **Patrick C. Shine,** a prominent lawyer of Spokane. Washington, in 1909, is the only person of that name I know of in that state; no doubt there are others living there. Patrick C. Shine is a descendant of the family Shine mentioned in a previous chapter of this work. In a letter dated March 19, 1907, to the author, Mr. Shine gives so clear and concise a statement of his people that I reproduce it.

"My father's name was **Michael Shine**; his forefathers for ages lived on the same farm he owned at Dirreen, in the Parish of Athea, in the County of Limerick. Being a very prolific race, noted principally for longevity, many of the family had to scatter, as only one son, generally the eldest, got the fortune on the farm. My father had six brothers: John, a village shopkeeper at Athea; Daniel and Cornelus, who died in the London Constabulary; Bartholomew and Frank, lawyers, Dublin, and Edmond, who came to America, whose son, John E. Shine, your namesake, is now general passenger and ticket agent of the S. P., at Kansas City, Mo. He has, like myself, numerous brothers and sisters in Kansas City.

"Last year, on my way back from Europe, I met many Shines in Indianapolis, Ind., who lived in Kerry and Cork, and the old men knew my father and his brothers well and claimed second and third degree relationship.

"I am just in receipt of a letter from my sister, Katherine, from Brooklyn, N. Y. She has just completed a tour, and in describing Muckross Abby (Killarney), she says, Father Brosnan (our cousin from mother's side) took her to see the grave of one of her cousins. On the headstone she read: 'Owen Shine, age 117 yrs.,' etc. I had not heard of him.

"I was educated principally at Mungret College, Limerick (S. J.), matriculated from Civil Service Academy. Had a business career, bookkeeper there. Came to this country twenty-one years ago. Entered politics, was D. C.

71

Col., Jackson Co., Mo. Studied law there; went railroading; worked from the truck to traveling auditor; turned to law and politics again; served as counsel for O. K. & N. here, five years; have practiced here eight years. Will be glad to hear further from you.

Yours very truly,

P. C. Shine."

And again writing, August 26, 1909, he said:

"Upon my return from the Pacific coast, I find your favor. Also I am in receipt of a like one from J. J. Shine, Western Passenger Agent, Wabash Railroad Co., Kansas City, asking me to give you the information required in your letter.

"I am not in a position to give you correct information, but would refer you to the Parish record of Athea, County Limerick, Ireland.

"Your letter is somewhat late; had you written it to me a year ago, I could have obtained a great deal of information for you from my father, Michael Shine, of Direen, Athea, County Limerick, Ireland, who died about a year ago, at about the age of 95. Several of my aunts and uncles I never knew. We were related to the Burks and Kellys of Lilstowel, Co. Kerry, Ireland. My father's mother's name was Kelly. My mother's name was Helen Connors. Her people came from Islandanny, Abbeyfeale, Co. Limerick. Two of my uncles, Bartholomew Shine and Frank Shine, were law writers in the City of Dublin, but died young in the year of the plague. I have often heard the family mention Elizabeth Shine of the Barracks, west of Athea, who emigrated to the United States, and was the mother of David Farragut. I cannot say what relation existed between the two families, only that they were cousins."

Mr. Shine is one of the foremost lawyers in the State of Washington, and a prominent figure in politics on the Pacific slope.

The following clipping was taken from Dawson Daily News, Dec. 11, 1908, published at Dawson, Alaska, speaking of the stampede to a new stream on the Steward about ten miles below the mouth of the Black Hills:

"Tom Shine, an old timer about Dawson, is understood to be one of the stampeders. Wade, who worked a long time at the N. A. T., and another man are said to know something of the matter. They are leading the rush.

CHAPTER X.

THE SHINE FAMILY IN CALIFORNIA.

There are several families of the name Shine living in the State of California, but we are without data of them to enable more than mention:

243. Daniel Shine was in the bookbinding business on Fourteenth St., San Francisco, in 1905, and
244. Julia Shine had a position in the Government department there in 1905.
245. J. H. Shine, Sonora Tuolumine Co., living in 1898.

THE SHINE FAMILY IN MASSACHUSETTS.

246. John P. Shine, M. D., living at Holyoke, in 1906. His parents had resided there for many years and were one of the leading families of that place. Mr. Shine had several brothers and sisters. His youngest sister, Miss Honoria Kennelly Shine, graduated from Trinity College, Washington, D. C., in 1909.

SHINES IN KENTUCKY.

247. Judge Michael Shine resided at Covington, Ky., for many years, where he practiced law. He was one of the leading lawyers of the state. He held high office in A. O. H. Society, and was a prominent K. C., living in 1914.

CHAPTER XI.

Shine Family in Canada.

Daniel Shine.

248. **Daniel Shine** emigrated from Ireland in the early part of the nineteenth century, and settled in Smithstown, near Peterborough, Ontario. The name Smithstown has since been changed to Omenee. We designate him as the head of the family Shine in the Dominion of Canada. It may be possible that some member of the Shine family of Ireland settled in Canada before that time, but as we have no information of others of the name having settled there prior to that, we may content ourselves in saying he was the first of the name to settle in Canada.

I think there is no doubt that this is the same Daniel Shine that resided at Ballymichael, Ireland, and operated a flouring mill there, mention of which was made in a previous chapter. There are many circumstances that would seem convincing that he is one and the same person. People living in the vicinity of Ballymichael remember well hearing their parents and others speak of him as a man of great physique and a regular athlete. He was said to be the most powerful man in the whole country around there. The grandsons of the Daniel Shine who settled in Canada, say the same of him. The date of his emigration from Ireland corresponds closely with the time those at Ballymichael say he left there. It is said by some of the family that he came to Canada sometime before his family came out. It appears that the family came to Canada about the year 1823; while at Ballymichael, Ireland, it is generally understood that he came out about 1819, and possibly he came to this country four or five years in advance of his family, with a man by the name of Prossor. Some of his descendants say the oldest child, Mary, was 21 years "at the time," and the next oldest, a son, Michael, nineteen years. I assume they were referring to the time Daniel came out and not to the time the family emigrated. This, at least, corresponds with dates of subsequent events as to births and deaths. It is stated that Daniel Shine, the third child, died Jan. 23, 1888, aged 87 years. This would tend to fix the dates of the birth of the elder children to correspond with their ages given if their father came out in 1819, which we assume to be correct.

In Ballymichael it was thought that he went to Philadelphia with one Timothy Buckley. While in Canada he is understood as having come direct from Ireland to Smiths township, near Peterboro, Canada. These discrepancies may easily have arisen through misunderstanding or through fault of memory. There are circumstances too that would indicate that he may have been the Daniel Shine of Cooleen, in County Limerick, who settled at Ballymichael. His grandsons say they have heard him often say that he came from Cork County, Ireland. He often spoke of Mallow, Charleville, and other places in the county. He frequently mentioned his brothers, Thomas and John, that he left in Ireland, which corresponds with the brothers mentioned in the chapter Shines of Mallow, Ballyclough, Cooleen. He married Bridget Ellen (Nell) Sheehan, in Ireland, but I have been unable to find any baptismal record of the family in Ireland. Church records were not preserved as far back as would give that information. His family was young when he emigrated; Mary, the oldest, was 21 years; Michael, the oldest son, was 19 years. He settled on a farm in Smiths township, where he resided until the time of his death, about the year 1854, and where some of the family resided for a long time afterwards. He raised a large family of children, five sons and two daughters. His sons inherited his fine physique and athletic qualities and when grown to manhood were regarded as having the finest physique and were the ablest and best men in the neighborhood. His family and descendants are as follows:

248. Daniel Shine (1).

Daniel Shine was born in Ireland, in either the County Cork or Limerick County, about the year 1765. He married Bridget Ellen Sheehan, about 1795, and emigrated to Canada about the year 1819 or 1823. Their children were all born in Ireland and were:

249. (1) Mary Shine, born in about 1797; m. James Vanatten.
250. (2) Michael Shine, born in about 1799; m.
251. (3) Daniel Shine, born in about 1801; died Jan. 1888.

252. (4)   Dennis Shine, born in about the year ——.
253. (5)   John Shine.
254. (6)   Ellen Shine; m. —— Hogan; d., 1912.
255. (7)   William Shine.

SECOND GENERATION.

249. Mary Shine (2). Daniel Shine (1).

Mary Shine, the first child of Daniel Shine and Nell Shine, was born in Cork County, Ireland, about the year 1797. She emigrated to Canada with the others of the family about the year 1823. She married James Vanatten about the year 1827, and settled in Rochester, New York. They raised a large family, but I have been unable to get their names.

250. Michael Shine (2). Daniel Shine (1).

Michael Shine, the second child of Daniel Shine and Nell Shine, was born in County Cork, Ireland, about the year 1799, and emigrated to Canada with the others of the family about the year 1823. He married ——, about the year ——, and settled in Emily township, near Lindsay, Ont. He was a progressive farmer and built up a large and appointed farm at that place. Their children were:

256. (1)   William Shine, born 1830, lived at Brussels, Ont., had 11 children, 6 boys and 5 girls.
257. (2)   Daniel Shine, born 1832, living at Cadillac, Mich.
258. (3)   Michael Shine, born 18——, lives at Wiarton, Ont. They had 11 children, 5 boys and 6 girls.
259. (4)   Robert Shine, born 18——.
260. (5)   John Shine, born 18——, lives near Seney, Mich.
261. (6)   Samuel Shine, born 18——.
262. (7)   Tryphona, born 18——.
263. (8)   Agnes, born 18——.
264. (9)   Sevina, born 18——.
265. (10) Ellen, born 18——, living at Downeyville, Ont.

251. Daniel Shine (2). Daniel Shine (1).

Daniel Shine, the third child of Daniel Shine and Nell Shine, was born in County Cork, Ireland, about the year 1801, and emigrated to Canada with the others of the family about the year 1823. He married Ann Gallagher, about the year 1835, and settled near Lindsay, Ont., where he, owned a fine farm. Ann Gallagher was born in 1802, and died in 1900. Their children were:

266. (1) John Shine, born 1837; died 1861.
267. (2) James Shine, born 1839; enlisted as a volunteer in U.S. army, served five years, and in 1909, living on the old homestead in the township of Ops.
268. (3) Mary Ann Shine, born 1841; m. John Wynn; living in 1909, at Lindsay, Ont.
269. (4) William Shine, born 1844, a merchant in town of Staynor, Ont.
270. (5) Daniel Shine, born 1847, died 1859.
271. (6) Michael Shine, born 1849, died 1884.
272. (7) Thomas Shine, born 1852; living in 1909, at Lindsay, Ont.
273. (8) George Shine, born 1855; in 1913, living at West Branch, Mich.

252. Daniel Shine (2). Daniel Shine (1).

Dennis Shine, the fourth child of Daniel Shine and Nell Shine, was born in Cork County, Ireland, about the year 1803. He emigrated to Canada with the family about the year 1825. He married Bridget Soullivan, about the year 1840, and settled in Emily Township, near Lindsay, Ont. Their children were:

274. (1) John Shine.
275. (2) Eugene Shine, born 1843; living (1913) at Downeyville, Ont.
276. (3) William Shine.
277. (4) Dennis Shine.
278. (5) Ellen Shine.
279. (6) Julia Shine.
280. (7) Mary Shine.

281. (8) Isabell Shine.
282. (9) Kate Shine

275. Eugene Shine (3). Dennis Shine (2). Daniel Shine (1).

Eugene Shine, the second son of Dennis Shine and Bridget Soullivan, was born in the year 1843, at ——; married Mary Houlihan, in about the year 1870 and settled at Downeyville, Ontario. Their children were:

283. (1) Lillie Shine, born in the year 1871.
284. (2) Kate. Shine, born in the year 1872.
285. (3) Aggie Shine, born in the year 1874.
286. (4) Dennis Shine, born in the year 1875.
287. (5) William Shine, born in the year 1876.
288. (6) Maggie Shine, born in the year 1877.
289. (7) Mary Shine, born in the year 1879.
290. (8) Thresia Shine, born in the year 1881.
291. (9) Eugene Shine, born in the year 1889.

257. Daniel Shine (3). Michael Shine (2). Daniel Shine (1).

Daniel Shine, the second child of Michael Shine and ——, was born near Lindsay, Ont., about the year 1832. He married a ——. Cook and settled at Cadillac, Mich. (living there in 1913), and raised a large family, six boys and five girls.

273. George Shine (3). Daniel Shine (2). Daniel Shine (1).

George Shine, the eighth child of Daniel Shine and Ann (Gallagher) Shine, was born near Lindsay, Ont., in the year 1855. He married Margaret Finnegan, a daughter of Timothy Finnegan and Catherine O'Mahoney, of County Cork, Ireland. They were married at —— about the year 18——. He moved to Sault Ste. Marie, Michigan, in 1881. He engaged in farming there for a time, and then engaged in business in the city. In 1903, he sold out and moved to West Branch, Mich., where he purchased a farm, and now (in 1913) with his wife, still lives on and operates his farm. He has a large acquaintance where he lives and is regarded as one of the foremost men of the place. They have no children.

The Ontario branch of the family "Shine" are very prolific, of a sturdy race, with fine physique and strong intellect, and it is to be regretted that more data of them could not be secured.

SHINES AT SEAFORTH, ONT.

A family of Shines settled in McKillop Township, near Seaforth, Ont. They were said to be descendants of Thomas Shine, a brother of Daniel Shine, who settled at Smithstown. We have been unable to learn when they settled there, or their names, except William Shine, who had resided there for a long time, and his widow, Mrs. William Shine, was living there in 1909.

CHAPTER XII.

The Shine Family in Michigan.

15. John Shine of Port Austin, Michigan, Founder.

The ancestors of this branch of the Shine family was Thomas Shine, who married Mary Sheehan and resided at Ballyclough, near Mallow, Ireland. Their children were as before mentioned:

> Catherine, born Dec., 1821; m. Thomas Kiley; d. Jan. 16, 1911.
> **John**, born Sept. 27th, 1823; m. Catherine Moore; d. Feb. 4th, 1902.
> Daniel, born Aug., 1825; d. June, 1826.
> Margaret, born Jan., 1827; d. in infancy.
> Eliza, born Dec. 25th, 1828; m. Thomas Francis Gallagher; d. March 25, 1909.
> Mary, born Sept., 1830; m. John Starr; d. Nov. 27th, 1915.
> Ellen, born Aug., 1836; m. William King; d. May 14th, 1910.

15. John Shine (2). Thomas Shine (1).

John Shine, son of Thomas Shine and Mary Sheehan, of Ballyclough, Ireland, was the founder of the family of Michigan Shines. While others of the name Shine have resided in the state, their residence was but temporary, or of later years. John Shine, the founder of the family, settled at Port Crescent, in the Township of Hume, County of Huron, about the year 1863. Port Crescent, once an active business town, ceased to exist in the early '80's, and Port Austin, a nearby town, became the leading city of the place.

As we have seen, he was born at Ballyclough, near the City of Mallow, County Cork, Ireland, September 27th, 1823. His father, Thomas Shine, died about the year 1837. After finishing his education in the highest schools of the place, he went to England and Wales about the year 1840. In Wales he took up civil engineering and mechanics. He afterwards took charge of one of the large blast furnaces at Pontopool, Wales, and continued for several years in charge of it. About the year 1849, he went to France and assisted in surveying for the first railroad that was constructed from Marseilles to Paris. In the year 1851, he sailed for Quebec, Canada. He was in the employ of the Grand Trunk Railway Company, and came out in their employ. He was for a time connected with the contracting firm of Massey & Brassey. In coming to America, he came on the sailing ship, "Charles Sanders." She was five weeks crossing the ocean. She encountered very rough weather in crossing, and at one time some of her spars and rigging had to be cut away to free the ship.

JOHN SHINE.

After arriving at Quebec, he continued for a time with the Grand Trunk Railway Co., building railroads. He left the railroad business to take charge of the shipping of square timber from Quebec to foreign ports. The shipping of square timber at that time constituted one of the great industries of the place, there being employed, at times, as many as a thousand men at this work. He later became interested with Mr. John Moore, of Montreal, a successful contractor at that place. He had been a contractor in the erection of the Victoria Bridge over the St. Lawrence river. After continuing in the contracting work with Mr. Moore for a time, he again took up railroad work for the Grand Trunk Company, which was then building the St. Thomas and Hamilton branch of its line. He married Catherine Moore, at Danville, Canada, January 23, 1854. She was a daughter of Michael Moore and Hanora Moran, and a grandniece of John Moore, of Montreal, the contractor above mentioned.

Mr. Shine continued for several years in charge of the railroad work. He resided for a time at Hamilton, Oshwau, and Middleton Center (now Courtland), while in charge of the work. Finally, in 1857, he gave up railroad work and engaged in farming and mill work at Courtland until 1862, when he went to Michigan. The State at that time, in the eastern central part, was sparsely settled, and lumbering and the manufacture of forest products were the chief industries. During the summer of 1862, he had charge of the lumber mill of Mr. Belleau, at Kawkawlin, Mich. He only remained there one season, although Mr. Belleau offered every inducement for him to remain. In addition to the salary he was getting, Mr. Belleau offered him a section of pine timber lands and a plot of about three acres of land in what is now the center or heart of Bay City, Michigan, but as there was much malaria and sickness in the vicinity, he did not deem it advisable to remain there at that time. He returned to Courtland, Canada, and with his family moved to Port Austin, Mich., in the spring of 1863. There he took up mechanical engineering in the mills at Port Austin and Port Crescent. In 1864, he settled on a farm in Hume township nearby, but for several years continued mechanical engineering, after which time he devoted nearly all of his time to the improvement of his farm which was one of the finest in the county. He continued to reside on his farm until the time of his death, February 4th, 1902.

He was a man of medium height—5 feet, 8 or 9 inches—and weighed about 175 pounds. He was possessed of a wonderful constitution, great strength and endurance. He had scarcely ever known an ill day, and retained his strength and vitality to the last. He was a man of great intellect, and possessed an extraordinary memory. His powerful, black eyes, beneath a crag-like brow, gave a facial expression that assisted in carrying conviction to his utterances. He had great force of character and soon became a leading man in that part of the state.

When he settled in Michigan, that section of the country was a primeval forest, with all its virgin wilderness. There were but few settlers, and hamlets were miles apart. The environments were such as to bring forcibly to the front the strongest character of men. His high education, wide experience, his forcible manner, and high sense of justice soon made him one of the prominent men of the county. He held many offices of public trust in both the township and county, and had been closely connected with the development of that part of the state. He was known far and near, and loved and respected by all.

The following is taken from The Port Austin News of February 7th, 1902, and also from the Journal of The Cork Historical Archaeological Society, Vol. VIII, 2nd Series, at page 127:

"JOHN SHINE.
AN OLD PIONEER HAS PASSED AWAY.

John Shine, an old resident of Huron County, died at his farm home in Hume township, last Tuesday, February 4th, at the advanced age of 78 years, 4 months and 8 days, surrounded by the members of his family.

Mr. Shine was born at Ballyclough, Mallow, County of Cork, Ireland, September 27, 1823. He was the only surviving son of his parents, Thomas Shine and Mary Sheehan. His father died before Mr. Shine reached his majority, and his mother did not long survive. After finishing his education in the national schools of that place, he went to England and resided there and in Wales for several years, where he learned engineering, and became proficient as a machinist. He went from there to France in the latter part of the forties, where he was engaged in the survey of the railroad then in construction from Paris to Marseilles. He landed in Quebec, Canada, in May, 1851, after a long and stormy voyage across the ocean on the vessel Charles Saunders. He came out in the employ of the Grand Trunk Railway Co., and was engaged for several years in the construction and operation of railroads for the company near Quebec.

He was married to Catherine Moore, at Danville, Canada, January 23, 1854, who survives him. Six children were born to them, three boys and three girls, of whom five are living, Mrs. James T. McIlhargie and John W. Shine, of Sault Ste. Marie, Mich.; Thomas Shine, of Bad Axe, Mich.; Michael Shine, of Kinde, Mich., and Elizabeth Shine, residing with her parents. His oldest daughter, Mary Shine, was married to Martin Carmody, in 1870, and died in 1879. Four sisters, Mrs. Thomas Kiley, of Grand Rapids, Wis; Mrs. John Starr, of Washburn, Wis.; Mrs. King, of St. Louis, Mo., and Mrs. Gallagher, of Indianapolis, Ind., survive him. Mr. Shine was one of the early settlers in the northern portion of the Thumb of Michigan, having moved there with his family in 1863. At that time that section of Michigan was a primeval forest with but few settlers and without schools or churches. After locating in Michigan, he followed engineering at Port Austin and Port Crescent for four or five years, after which time he devoted almost his entire attention to the improvement of his farm which is one of the finest in the county, and where he resided up to the time of his death. Mr. Shine was a man of remarkable force of character. His high education, wide experience, wonderful memory and forcible manner and style of conversation made him one of the foremost men of the county. He was generous to a fault and his reputation for honesty and justice made him loved and respected by all. He held many offices of public trust in the county and has been closely connected with the growth and development of this section of the country. He was a strong, rugged man, and retained his strength and activity up to the time of his late illness, during which time he personally supervised the management of his farm. His death, although expected, was a great shock to his family and friends, as he had been ill for only about three weeks and confined to his bed about ten days before his death, which was the result of gangreous ulceration of his teeth. He passed to his reward peacefully and happy in the presence of his wife and children. His extraordinary faculties did not desert him and he remained conscious to the last, conversing with his family, and after saying a last good-bye, passed quietly away.

He was buried from St. Michael's Catholic church of this place, Thursday morning. High mass being said by Rev. Fr. Kolkiewicz, assisted by Fr. Dunnegan, of Argyle, who also delivered an impressive sermon. The funeral services were attended by a large concourse of friends and neighbors and the remains were carried to their last resting place by the following old settlers of the neighborhood and county: Philip Carrol, M. Fremont, Robert McAlister, Wm. Etzler, Thos. Welsh, and James Grannell."

SHINEVALE FARM.

Catherine Moore Shine, wife of John Shine, of Port Austin, was, as we have seen, born December 25th, 1823, at Ballylongford, County Kerry, Ireland. She was a daughter of Michael Moore and Hanora Moran Moore. Her father, Michael Moore, was of the famous Moore family of ancient Kerry. Her mother, Honora Moran Moore, was, on her mother's side, of the Scanlan branch of the noted Geraldines of Kerry. She was blessed with a perfect form and a graceful mind, and, when a girl, was said to be "the most beautiful girl in the Kingdom of Kerry." The family came from Ireland to Montreal, Canada, in the year 1851.

Catherine Moore Shine, inherited many of the charms and characteristics of her mother. She, too, was of graceful form and charming manners, and a beautiful woman. When a girl on the banks of the Shannon, she was popularly known as "Kitty Moore," and was a great favorite with all, both rich and poor. In womanhood she was loved and respected by all wherever she resided. She was of great assistance to Mr. Shine, and his success in life was due in part to her. She always possessed the best of health, and retained her strength and vitality up to the time of her death. She died July 21st, 1909, at the advanced age of 85 years.

CATHERINE MOORE SHINE.

A short sketch of her life, as appeared in The Independent Farmer at the time of her death, is reproduced as follows:

"DEATH OF MRS. SHINE.

Pioneer of Hume Township and Well Known
Woman Died Suddenly.

Mrs. Catherine Shine, an old resident of Hume Township, died at the family home at Shinevale Farm, Wednesday July 21st, after a very short illness.

Mrs. Shine was a daughter of Michael and Hanora Moore, and was born at Ballylongford, Ireland, Dec. 24th, 1823, and was 85 years, 6 months and 27 days old at the time of her death. She came to Montreal, Canada, with her brothers, in the year 1851, and was married to her late husband, John Shine, at Danville, Canada, January 23rd, 1854. She continued to reside in Canada, where Mr. Shine was engaged in railroad construction, until the year 1863, when the family moved to Port Crescent, and in 1864, on the farm known as Shinevale Farm, where she resided until the time of her death.

Mrs. Shine had five brothers and one sister. Three of her brothers and her sister, with their parents, came from Ireland about the same time, and of this family there is now but one survivor, Mrs. Daniel Ahearn, of Hume. Her mother died in 1876, at the age of 83, and is buried in the Catholic cemetery at Port Austin. Mrs. Shine, on her mother's side, was a descendant of the Geraldines, a family of great distinction in Irish history.

In her girlhood years she was one of the most popular young ladies in the parish where she lived. Her frank, natural disposition, cheerful and generous manner, with her loving and amiable character, which made her so many friends in her younger years, remained with her through life and endeared her to all who knew her. Her cheerful disposition, and motherly love did much towards making the family home a place of real enjoyment, not only for the members of her family, but for all her friends and neighbors, who always received a very hearty welcome from her at her home.

Mrs. Shine was a woman of exceptionally good health, scarcely ever having any sickness. She retained her physical vigor and mental faculties up until the end. She died of acute indigestion and was apparently in her usual health a few minutes before she passed away.

She survived her husband about seven years, and of her six children, five survive her, Thomas Shine of Bad Axe, Mich., Mrs. J. T. McIlhargie and John W. Shine, of Sault Ste. Marie, Mich., and Elizabeth Shine and Michael Shine at home.

She was interred in the Port Austin Catholic cemetery, on July 23rd, Rev. Father Plagens officiating. The funeral was one of the largest seen in years, and many of her old friends and neighbors paid their last respects to her that was so dear to them for many years. The pall bearers were: James Grannell, John Cummings, James Ahearn, Richard Clancy, Edward Ahearn and Frank Etzler."

The children of John Shine and Catherine Moore Shine were:

292.   (1)   Mary Shine, born at Hamilton, Ontario, Nov. 29th, 1854; married Martin Carmody, Sept., 1870; had five children, four boys and one girl; died March 4th, 1879.

293. (2)   Nora Shine, born at Ashwa, Ont., Aug. 7th, 1856; married J. Thomas McIlhargie, Feb. 24th, 1876; had three children, two boys and one girl.

294. (3)   Thomas Shine, born at Courtland (then Middleton Center), Ont., January 23rd, 1858; married Ann McAlister, June 29th, 1887; had six children, three boys and three girls.

295. (4)   Elizabethe Shine, born at Courtland (then Middleton Center), Ont., Dec. 7th, 1859; not married.

296. (5)   John W. Shine, born at Courtland (then Middleton Center), Ont., April 8th, 1861; not married.

297. (6)   Michael Shine, born at Courtland (then Middleton Center), Ont., June 24th, 1862; married Sarah Neph, Jan., 1888; had one child, Vera, born in June, 1890; his wife, Sarah, died Jan. 12th, 1891. He married Mary McGuire in June, 1894; she died Jan. 20th, 1907. They had eight children, seven of which, five boys and two girls, are living.

The children of Michael Moore and Hanora Moran Moore were:

298. (1)   Patrick, born 1818; m. Mary O'Marra; lived at Montreal, Canada; died Nov. 29th, 1893.

299. (2)   Michael, born 1820; single; died at England, Oct., 1852.

300. (3)   Catherine, born Dec. 24th, 1823; m. John Shine at Danville, Ga., in 1854; lived at Port Austin, Mich.; died July 21st, 1909.

301. (4)   John, born 1826; single; died Jan. 12th, 1901.

302. (5)   Edward, born 1829; married Margaret Tehan, 1857; lived at Bay Port and Pinnebog, Mich.; d. Jan., 1906.

303. (6)   Thomas, and

304. (7)   Morris, twins, born 1832; died 1832.

305. (8)   Thomas, born 1834; died 1853.

306. (9)   Johana, born Nov. 15th, 1838; married Daniel Ahearn; lived at Port Austin, Mich.

14. Catherine Shine (2). Thomas Shine (1).

Catherine Shine, daughter of Thomas Shine and Mary Sheehan, as we have seen, was born at Ballyclough, Ireland, in the year 1821. She was the oldest of the family, and in about the year 1840, with her mother and three sisters, came to Quebec, Canada. She married Thomas Kiley, at Quebec, Aug. 28th, 1848. In 1856, they moved to Milwaukee, Wis. They finally settled at Grand Rapids, Wisconsin, in the year 1865, where Mr. Kiley engaged in the shoe business. Their children were:

307. (1) Catherine, born at Quebec, 1849; m. —— Houghton; living at ——.
308. (2) Thomas Kiley, born.
309. (3) William Kiley, born ——; d. 1882.
310. (4) George Kiley, born ——.

Catherine Shine was an exceptionally bright woman. Her snapping black eyes harmonized well with her forcible character. She was a very charitable person and a great favorite where she lived. She died January 16th, 1911, at the advanced age of 90 years. Her husband, Thomas Kiley, was born at Waterford, Ireland, March 12th, 1907, and died at Grand Rapids, Wis., July 4th, 1904, at the age of 97 years.

18. Eliza Shine (2). Thomas Shine (1).

Eliza Shine, daughter of Thomas Shine and Mary Sheehan, was born at Ballyclough, Mallow, Ireland, December 25th, 1828. She came to Quebec with her mother and sisters, about 1840. She married Thomas Francis Gallagher, at Quebec, June 25th, 1855, where they resided for several years. In 1860, they moved to St. Louis, Mo., where Mr. Gallagher engaged in building contract work. Their children were:

311. (1) Alice A., born at Quebec, Can., April 1, 1856; married Erick Z. Banks at Covington, Ky., Oct. 27, 1885. Settled at Indianapolis in 1896. He died ——, 19——. Their children were:
Paul, born at Covington, July 25, 1886; died 1886.
Leo, born at Covington, Nov. 25, 1889.
Alice Louise, born at. Covington, May 7, 1891.

312. (2) Mary, born at Quebec, Can., 1857; died Nov. 4, 1890; married John H. Pedell at St. Louis, in 1875; he died in 1892. Their children were:

John and Bessie. Both died in infancy.

313. (3) Amelia, born at St. Louis, 1861; died 1861.

314. (4) Bessie, born at St. Louis, 1865 married Robert Hawkins at Covington, Oct. 27, 1889; died at Indianapolis, 1903. Their children were:

Bessie, born at Covington, Aug. 8, 1890.

Ruth, born at Indianapolis, Sept. 10, 1892; married Cloyde Reber Fisher, at Indianapolis, Jan. 10, 1917.

315. (5) John, born at St. Louis, June 5, 1867; died Aug. 15, 1867.

ELIZA SHINE GALLAGHER.

Mr. Gallagher died about the year 1872, at Memphis. Mrs. Gallagher and family moved to Covington, Ky., about the year 1880, where they resided until the year 1896, when they moved to Indianapolis, Ind.

Eliza Shine Gallagher was an exceptionally handsome woman, and of striking appearance. She inherited the forcible characteristics of the Shine family, and was possessed of good health and great vitality. She died March 25, 1909, at the age of 80 years. No finer tribute could be paid any one than was written of her after her death by her daughter, Alice, in a letter written June 29th, 1909. She said:

> "She was a woman of distinguished appearance and manner; very beautiful; shining black hair, a little white at the temples; eyes, deep, dark and brilliant, and the complexion of a girl; small, beautifully shaped hands and feet—the rose flush remained frozen on her cheeks after death, and a singular look of early youth and a singular look of everlasting peace came over her face.***As she lay on her funeral couch she looked like some grand old Queen who had lain down to rest a while—friends who came to see her held their breath and said, 'If this is death, 'tis beautiful to die.'"

19. Mary Shine (2). Thomas Shine (1).

Mary Shine, the sixth child and third daughter of Thomas Shine and Mary Sheehan, was born at Ballyclough, Mallow, Ireland, in September, 1830. The records obtained did not give the date of her baptism, but her sister, Catherine Shine, the oldest of the family, in a letter written in 1909, referring to her age, said:

> "She was born one year and nine months after Eliza was born."

And as the records show that Eliza was born December 25th, 1828, the date of Mary's birth is fixed as September, 1830. She, with the other members of the family, came to Quebec about the year 1840. It was generally said by her older brother and sisters that she was about 10 years old when they came from Ireland. After her mother died, she lived with her sister, Catherine, until she married John Starr, at Quebec, Canada, about the year 1851. Soon after they were married, they moved to Wisconsin and finally settled at Grand Rapids, Wis., about the year 1855, where Mr. Starr engaged in farming and the lumber business. Their children were:

316. (1) James, born at ——, 1858; living at Washburn, Wis.
317. (2) John, born at ——, 1860; living at Washburn, Wis.
318. (3) Marie, born at ——, 1862; married John Graham at ——, in 1888; had —— children; now living at Washburn, Wis.
319. (4) Ellen, born at ——, 1864; married Peter Lebrash, at ——, in 1888; died ——.
320. (5) William, born at ——, 1870; living at ——.
321. (6) Thomas, born at ——, 1874; died 18——.
322. (7) Edward, born at Grand Rapids, 1878; died 18——.

About the year 1885, the family moved to Washburn, Wis., where they engaged in the hotel business. Her husband, John Starr, died at Ann Arbor, Michigan, where he went for treatment, January 11, 1900. And she died at Washburn, Nov. 27th, 1915, at the age of 85 years. She was the last of the family to go. Her sisters and brother had passed away before her. They were a remarkable family for their vitality and endurance. They were all blessed with good health and robust constitution. She was fair of complexion, and a very lovely woman. The Washburn News, in referring to her death, said:

> "Mrs. Starr was a kind, motherly lady, beloved by all who knew her. Her deeds of kindness were many. She was the first member of the pioneer association of Washburn, when that organization was formed, and she never failed to attend any function given by that organization. She will be missed in the community, but she leaves behind kind deeds that will ever be remembered."

She was buried in Woodland Cemetery, in the family lot, where Mr. Starr, and her sons, Thomas and Edward, and her daughter, Mrs. LeBrash, are buried.

20. Ellen Shine (2). Thomas Shine (1).

Ellen Shine, the seventh and youngest child of Thomas Shine and Mary Sheehan, was born at Ballyclough, Mallow, Ireland, in August, 1836. She, as a child, came with the family to Quebec about the year 1840. After her mother's death, she lived with her sister, Catherine, until she married. She married William King, at about the year 18—— They lived at ——, until they moved to St. Louis, Mo., in the year 18......, where Mr. King engaged in ——. He died in 1892, and she died at St. Louis, May 14th, 1910. Their children were:

323. (1) Mary, born at ——, 18——; died 18——.
324. (2) Ellen, born at ——, 18——; died 18——.
325. (3) William, born at ——, 18——; died 18——.
326. (4) John, born at ——, 18——; married ——, 18——; living at ——.
327. (5) Jennie, born at ——, 18——; married —— Hunt, 18——, at St. Louis; he died 1917. Their children were:

Ellen Shine was also of the brunette type; she had the deep, black eyes so characteristic of the family. She was a kind mother, and her daughter, Jennie, inherited many of her loving traits.

Johanna Moore.

Johanna Moore the eighth and youngest child of Michael Moore and Hanora Moran, was born at Ballylongford, County Kerry, Ireland, November 15th, 1838. She married Daniel Ahearn, at Tarbert, in 1853, and they went to England to live. She came to America in 1856, landing at Montreal, Canada. They lived at Middleton Center, now Courtland, Ontario, for a short time, and in 1860, moved to Port Austin, Michigan, where they settled on the farm where she now lives, in 1917. The country was new at that time and settlements were far apart, but Mr. Ahearn built up one of the best farms in the vicinity; and continued to manage it until the time of his death in 19——.

Their children were:

1. Nora, born at Middleton Center, Ont., June, 1858; living with her mother at the farm.

2. Edward, born at Middleton Center, Ont., 18——; married Anna Bruce at Port Austin, 18——; have —— children, —— boys and —— girls; living at Kinde, Mich.
3. John, born at Port Austin, Mich., 18——; died 18——.
4. Minnie, born at Port Austin, Mich., 18——.
5. James, born at Port Austin, Mich., 18——; married Alice Neph, at Port Austin, 18——; had —— children, —— boys and —— girls; resides at Kinde, Mich.
6. Daniel, born at Port Austin, Mich., 18——; living at Emmet, Mich.
7. Michael, born at Port Austin, 18——; living at old home.
8. Thomas, born at Port Austin, 18——; living at old home.
9. Patrick, born at Port Austin, 18——; died ——, 18——.
10. Anna, born at Port Austin, 18——; married Frank McGuire, at Port Austin, in 1916; living at Port Austin.
11. Frank, born at Port Austin, 1882; died Dec. 25, 1908.
12. Nellie, born at Port Austin, 1888; living at Detroit.

Edward Moore.

Edward Moore, the fifth child of Michael Moore and Hanora Moran, was born at Ballylongford, County Kerry, Ireland, in the year 1829. He, with his brother, Patrick, and sister, Catherine, came to Montreal in 1852. He married Margaret Tehan, at Montreal, in 1856, and moved to Michigan in 1860. They settled for a short time at Port Austin, and in 1862, moved to Bay Port, Michigan, where he engaged in farming. He built up a fine farm in the virgin forest there. In 1875, he sold his farm and moved to Meade Tps., and purchased a farm in the township of Meade, near Pinnebog, where he remained until his death in 19——Mrs. Moore died ——, 1906.

Their children were:

1. Patrick, born at ——, March 17th, 1857, married Mary Robinson, at Munissing, Mich., 18——; living at Los Angeles, California. They have three children, one boy and   two girls, Frank, Edna and Beatrice.
2. Michael, born at ——, 18——; living at Felion, Mich.

3. Joseph, born at Middleton Center, now Courtland, Ont., 18——; living at Seattle, Wash.

4. John, born at Bay Port, Mich., ——, 18——; married Mary Bliss, at ——, 18——; had two children, Ray and Hazen; now living at Detroit, Mich.

5. Thomas, born at Bay Port, Mich., 18——; married ——, 18——; had five children, two girls and three boys. His wife died ——, 19—— He married second wife, ——, 19—— He has been a resident of Montreal since 18——.

6. Lenore, born at Bay Port, Mich., ——, 18——; taught school many years; moved to Seattle Wash., in 19——; died at Seattle, Dec. 29th, 19——.

7. James, born at Bay Port, Mich., 18——; moved to Seattle, 19——

8. Frank, born at Bay Port, Mich., 18——; died 1895.

9. Kathleen, born at Bay Port, 18——; went to Los Angeles, 19——; married —— Wadell, at ——, 18——; living at ——.

10. Maggie, born at Bay Port, Mich., 18——; living at ——.

292. Mary Shine (3). John Shine (2). Thomas Shine (1).

Mary Shine, the oldest child of John Shine and Catherine Moore, was born at Hamilton, Ont., November 29th, 1854. She came to Port Austin, Michigan, with her parents in 1863. She married Martin Carmody, at Port Austin, Mich., Sept. ——, 1870. He was a son of Patrick Carmody and Nellie Hogan. Mary Shine and her husband resided on a farm, in Hume Township, about two miles from her old home. She was of medium size, dark eyes and hair, mild disposition and a lovely person. She died at their farm home, March 4th, 1879.

Their children were:

328. (1) Patrick J., born Oct. 12th, 1871; resided at Kewatin, Minn.; died at the Rood Hospital, at Hibbing, Minn. February 18th, 1914, buried at Port Austin Cemetery.

329. (2) John, born 1873; died 1873.

330. (3) Michael, born Sept. 10, 1874, living at Filion, Mich.

331. (4) Nellie, born August 23rd, 1876; married George Deegan, May 26th, 1915; living at Port Austin, Mich.

332. (5) Martin, born February 23rd, 1879; went to Alberta, Can., 19——; residing near Empress, Alberta, Canada.

MARY SHINE.

293. Nora Shine (3). John Shine (2). Thomas Shine (1).

Nora Shine, the second oldest child of John Shine and Catherine Moore, was born at Ashawa, Ontario, August 7th, 1856. She came with her parents to Port Austin, Michigan, in 1863. She married J. Thomas McIlhargie, at Port Austin, February 24th, 1876. They resided on a farm in Lake Township, on the banks of the river Pinnebog, near the village of Pinnebog, Huron County, Mich., until the year 1884, when they engaged in the general mercantile business at Port Austin, Mich. In 1894, they moved to Newberrv, Michigan, where they resided until 1899, when they moved to Sault Ste. Marie, Mich. Mr. McIlhargie was superintendent of the waterworks of that city.

NORA SHINE

Nora Shine was of fair complexion, medium height, and mild disposition. She advanced rapidly at school and graduated as a teacher when only seventeen years of age. She taught school successfully for a number of years in the County of Huron, before her marriage. In later years she has taken a leading part in reading clubs and other societies.

Their children were:

333. (1) Herbert, born Feb. 2nd, 1877: living at Newberrv, Mich.
334. (2) Casper H., born Oct. 14th, 1878; married Philamene Schneider, at Sault Ste. Marie, May 6th, 1908; have two children, Edward, born Feb. 4th, 1912; John, born Nov. 2nd, 1913; living at Detroit, Mich.
335. (3) Edna M., born Oct. 4th, 1880; married Earl Ryan, August 7th, 1907; settled at Cass City, Mich., where Mr. Ryan engaged in the drug business. In 1902, sold out and moved to Detroit and engaged in the drug business, on Woodward avenue.

294. Thomas Shine (3). John Shine (2). Thomas Shine (1).

Thomas Shine, the third child of John Shine and Catherine Moore, was born at Middleton Center, now Courtland, Ontario, June 23rd, 1858. He came with his parents to Port Austin, Michigan, in 1863. He married Ann McAlister, daughter of Robert McAlister and Rebecca Clark, at Port Austin, June 29th, 1887. They resided on the Kennedy farm, near Port Crescent, for several years. They moved to their own farm in Hume Township, in the year 1895, where they resided until the year 1900, when they moved to Bad Axe, Michigan, the county seat, where he engaged in the implement business, and later in contract work. He opened up several large county drains in the County of Huron. Mrs. Shine died April 9th, 1907, at their home at Bad Axe, Mich., and was buried in the Bad Axe Cemetery.

Their children were:

336. (1) Grace, born April 18th, 1888; died April 30th, 1908.
337. (2) Elizabeth, born August 9th, 1889; died March 12th, 1907.
338. (3) John R., born June 11th, 1893.
339. (4) Edward, born March 18th, 1895.
340. (5) Maryetta, born June 18th, 1899.
341. (6) R. William, born April 1st, 1901.

THOMAS SHINE.

Thomas Shine was a man of more than ordinary height, he stood five feet, eleven inches, without shoes on, and weighed about 175 pounds. He was possessed of extraordinary strength, and was a perfect athlete in his younger days. His complexion was slightly dark, with dark, curly hair. His high sense of justice and fair dealing made him a great favorite among his acquaintances. He is now living at Bad Axe.

295. Elizabeth E. Shine (3). John Shine (2). Thomas Shine (1).

Elizabeth Shine, the fourth child of John Shine and Catherine Moore, was born at Middleton Center, now Courtland, Ontario, December 7th, 1859. She came with her parents to Port Austin, Michigan, in 1863, and lived with them at the old home—Shinevale—and was of great comfort and assistance to them in their old age. After finishing her education she graduated as a teacher, and taught in the public schools of Huron County for upwards of thirty years. She taught school at Meade, Hume, Dwight, Lincoln, Sheridan and Sigel. She was a handsome girl, with brown eyes and beautiful auburn hair. She inherited the constitution and vitality of the Shine family, and enjoyed the blessing of good health. She possessed great intellectual ability, and her generous disposition made her a favorite with all. After the death of her eldest sister, and her brothers' wives, she cared for and practically raised all the younger children. She was as a mother to them all. In her educational and charitable work she has been identified with the growth, and development of that part of the country, and enjoys a wide acquaintance in the State.

ELIZABETH SHINE.

296. John W. Shine (3). John Shine (2). Thomas Shine (1).

John W. Shine, the fifth child of John Shine and Catherine Moore, was born in Middleton Center, now Courtland, Ontario, April 8th, 1861. He came to Port Austin, Michigan, with his parents in 1863, and spent his early life on his father's farm, near that place. He received his early education at the schools at Port Crescent, Mich. He spent a year at Grand Rapids, Wisconsin, in the year 1882-83, where he held a position in the lumbering business with a Mr. Edwards, of Pt. Edwards. In the year 1884, he engaged in the general mercantile business at Port Austin, Mich., and continued in that business until 1887, when he took up the study of law. In June, 1888, he settled at Sault Ste. Marie, Michigan, where he entered the law office of Mr. M. J. Doyle. He was admitted to the bar in March, 1890, and immediately engaged in the practice of his profession at that place. He was City Attorney for the City of Sault Ste. Marie, in the years 1892, 1893, 1899, 1900 and 1901, during which time he framed many of the laws and ordinances of the city.

In the year 1900, he compiled the laws and ordinances of the city of Sault Ste. Marie, and they were published under his directions, making the most complete compilation in use in any city of the State. He built up a large and lucrative practice in his profession, and became one of the leading lawyers in the State. He was engaged in many important cases in both the State and Federal Courts. He represented the City of Sault Ste. Marie successfully before the Supreme Court, at Washington, in a suit to determine the right of the State of Michigan to regulate and fix the rate of ferriage in the St. Mary's River, an international boundary stream. The case was a very important one as it involved the rights of nearly every State in the Union.

Mr. Shine was strongly mentioned for the Federal Judgeship in the proposed new Judicial District for the Upper Peninsula of Michigan. The Evening News, published at Sault Ste. Marie, in referring to the proposed district, said:

> "It will require an Act of Congress to create the new district, and it is understood that a movement is on foot to get it through the present Congress. If a new district is created, the appointment will undoubtedly go to John W. Shine, of this city. Mr. Shine stands high with the present administration, and his appointment would be looked upon with favor. His long

practice in the United States Courts has well qualified him for the position, and he is recognized by his party as the logical candidate for the position."

The Detroit Journal said:

"The Upper Peninsula has such strong hopes that will be made into a distinct United States district that John W. Shine, of Sault Ste. Marie, is being boomed by his friends for appointment as U.S. District Judge when the new district is created by Congress. Mr. Shine was a former resident of Huron County, in the Thumb, and still operates a farm there."

JOHN W. SHINE.

Similar expressions of Mr. Shine's high standing appeared in the Huron County Tribune, the Port Austin News and many other papers in the state.

He was a delegate to the National Democratic Convention, held at St. Louis, in June, 1916, at which President Wilson was renominated for President of the United States.

At the Democratic State Convention, held at Grand Rapids, Michigan, in February, 1917, Mr. Shine was nominated for Justice of the Supreme Court of Michigan. Mr. Shine had not sought the nomination, but it came to him as a distinct recognition of his high standing in the legal profession.

The Huron County Tribune said:

> "John W. Shine, of the 'Soo,' brother of Thomas Shine, of this city, and former Huron County Attorney, is one of the nominees on the State Democratic ticket for Supreme Court Judge. Mr. Shine is of the very highest type of lawyer and citizen, and excellent timber for this position."

The State, however, being overwhelmingly Republican, the Democratic ticket was not successful.

297. Michael Shine (3). John Shine (2). Thomas Shine (1).

Michael Shine, the sixth and youngest child of John Shine and Catherine Moore, was born at Middleton Center, now Courtland, Ontario, June 24th, 1862. He came to Port Austin, Michigan, with his parents in 1863. He received his early education in the Port Crescent schools, and spent his early life on his father's farm, near Port Austin, Michigan. He married Sarah Neph, daughter of Jacob Neph and Mary Kelley, at Port Austin, in January, 1888, and settled at Kinde, Michigan, where he engaged in the hotel business. His wife died January 12th, 1891. They had one child, Vera, born in June, 1890. She married Robert O'Malley, August 12th, 1910; living at Detroit, Mich.

Michael Shine married his second wife, Mary McGuire, daughter of James McGuire and Mary Boyle, at Port Austin, June, 1894. They settled on a farm on the State Road, two miles north of Kinde. She died January 20th, 1907.

Their children were:

(1)   James Emmet, born August 1st, 1895.
(2)   John Bryan, born September 12th, 1896.
(3)   Frank, born November, 1898.
(4)   George, born February, 1900.
(5)   Annie, born April 28th, 1901.
(6)   Elizabeth, April 1st, 1903.
(7)   Daniel, January 20th, 1906.

MICHAEL SHINE.

Michael Shine was of more than average size. He was 5 feet 11 inches, without shoes, and weighed about 180 pounds in athletic form. He was of fair complexion, dark hair, and of fine physique.

CHAPTER XIII.

OTHER PERSONS OF THE NAME "SHINE" IN AMERICA.

Rev. C. L. Shyne, S. J., at St. Marys, Kansas.

Rev. M. J. Shine, at Middletown, N. Y., in 1905.

Rev. Michael A. Shine, at Plattsmouth, Neb., in 1912.

Rev. Eugene Shine, New York City, in 1910.

John E. Shine, Gen. Passenger Agent, Kansas City, Mo.

John Shine, Policeman, Chicago, Ill.

Joseph J. Shine, Policeman, Port Huron, Mich., in 1915.

John L. Shine, at the head of "Shine's Peerless Pierrots, Society Entertainers," at Detroit, in 1915.

Cornelius Shine, Chicago, 1907.

Daniel Shine, Chicago, 1907.

Daniel J. Shine, Chicago, 1907.

Daniel W. Shine, Chicago, 1907.

D. Joseph Shine, Jr., Chicago, 1907.

Frank D. Shine, Chicago, 1907.

Frederick Shine, Chicago, 1907.

John Shine, Chicago, 1907.

John J. Shine, Chicago, 1907.

John M. Shine, Chicago, 1907.

Joseph Shine, Chicago, 1907.

Joseph Shine, Chicago, 1907.

Joseph Shine, Chicago, 1907.

Lillian Shine, Chicago, 1907.

Margaret Shine, Chicago, 1907.

Martin E. Shinc, Chicago, 1907.

Mary E. Shine, Chicago, 1907.

Michael Shine, Chicago, 1907.

Michael G. Shine, Chicago, 1907.

Nathan Shine, Chicago, 1907.

Patrick Shine, Chicago, 1907.

Patrick J. Shine, Chicago, 1907.

William T. Shine, Chicago, 1907.

William F. Shine, Chicago, 1907.

William P. Shine, Chicago, 1907.

B. B. Shine, Green Bay, Wis, 1909.

Morris Shine, Drummond Island, Mich., 1914.

Miss Katie I. Shine, Lynchburg, Va., 1911.

John Alfred Shine, Lynchburg, Va., 1911.

Elizabeth Shine, Detroit, Mich., in 1910.

James Shine, Detroit, Mich., in 1910.

Margaret Shine, Detroit, Mich., in 1910.

Bart. J. Shine, Cincinnati, Ohio, 1910.

Bert Shine, Cincinnati, Ohio, 1910.

Edward shine, Cincinnati, Ohio, 1910.

James Shine, Cincinnati, Ohio, 1910.

James F. Shine, Cincinnati, Ohio, 1910.

John Shine, Cincinnati, Ohio, 1910.

John Shine, Cincinnati, Ohio, 1910.

John J. Shine, Cincinnati, Ohio, 1910.

Matt Shine, Cincinnati, Ohio, 1910.

Nora Shine, Cincinnati, Ohio, 1910.

Robert Shine, Cincinnati, Ohio, 1910.

Edward Shine, 57 Fulton St., Pittsburg, Pa. 1910.

R. Edgar Shine, Richmond, Va.

CHAPTER XIV.

WILL.

PUBLIC RECORD OFFICE OF IRELAND

Certified Copy of
A Record in the Public Record Office of Ireland,
Entitled:
Will of Elizabeth Lillis, 1836, Prerogative Court.

This is the last Will and Testament of me, **Elizabeth Lillis**, of Charleville, in the County of Cork Widow. Whereas, by indented deed, bearing date the thirty-first day of August, one thousand eight hundred and twenty-three, certain premises therein more particularly mentioned and described were granted and released unto James Curtin, party thereto, upon the trusts therein mentioned and during the continuance of a copartnership pursuant to the conditions of a deed of copartnership thereupon made and executed. And whereas, under and by virtue of the said deeds of release and copartnership I was entitled to one-third part or share of and in the capital and stock in the trade or business of tanner which has been heretofore carried on in Charleville aforesaid, in pursuance of the said deed of copartnership whereout I have already received the sum of one thousand seven hundred pounds. And under and by virtue of the said deed of release, I am possessed of a **freehold interest for lives renewable forever** in two houses called Conner's Plot, in the said town of Charleville, which are marked No. 1 in the map annexed to an Indenture of Lease, made to me by the late Wills George Crofts. And it is by said deed of release declared that the said two houses are free of all head and chief rent whatsoever. And whereas I am also possessed of a **freehold interest** in one small house in **Baker's Lane,** in Charleville aforesaid, which I hold of the representatives of the late Mary Roche. I give, devise and bequeath all the **freehold property** whereof I am now seized and possessed with its appurtenances unto **Daniel Murphy,** of the City of Cork, Merchant, and

Charles James Curtin, of **Mallow,** Doctor of Medicine, their heirs and assigns to have and to hold the same upon **trust** for the sole and separate **use** of my daughter, **Margt. Cahill,** her heirs and assigns, free from the debts, controul or intermeddling of her husband. I give and bequeath to the said **Daniel Murphy** and **Charles James Curtin,** their executors and adms., the sum of **one thousand pounds,** to hold the same in trust for the sole use and benefit of my said daughter, **Margaret Cahill,** her exors. and admors., free from the debts, controul or intermeddling of her husband. I give and bequeath to **Michael Sarsfield,** of the town of Charleville, the husband of my deceased daughter, Mary, the sum of **one hundred pounds;** to my nephew, **Daniel Shine,** the sum of **one hundred pounds.** I give to my sister, **Catherine Shine,** the sum of **fifty pounds,** and in case the decease of my said sister shall occur prior to my own, then I give and bequeath the said sum of fifty pounds to Ellen, the daughter of my said sister, Catherine. To **Sarah Catherine** and **John Shine,** the children of my nephew, **John Shine, I** give the sum of **one hundred pounds,** to be divided amongst them, share and share alike, when and as they shall respectively attain their ages of twenty-one years and from the time of my decease I desire that the interest upon their respective portions shall accumulate for their benefit and if either of them shall die before attaining her or his age of twenty-one years, then I desire that the share or portion of her or him so dying, with the interest thereon, shall be paid to the survivors, share and share alike, at their respective ages of twenty-one years, and if only one of them survives, then the whole, with the interest thereon, to be paid to such survivor at his or her age of twenty-one years. I give and bequeath to the said **Danl. Murphy,** his Exeors. and Admors., the sum of **one hundred pounds** upon **trust** to pay the same at the rate of ten pounds yearly with the interest thereon to my said daughter, **Margaret Cahill,** to be by her distributed for the use and benefit and for the clothing and other necessary wants of the most destitute and distressed children in the National poor school of Charleville. I give and bequeath to the religious society, called the **Sisters of Charity,** the sum of **fifty pounds,** to be paid to that part of their association that shall be established in Charleville. And as to all the **residue** and **remainder** of my property, real, freehold and personal, not hereinbefore and hereby disposed of, I give, devise and bequeath the same to the said **Daniel Murphy** and **Charles James Curtin,** and the survivor of them, his heirs, exeors. and admors., upon trust for the sole **use** and **benefit** of my said daughter, **Margaret Cahill,** her heirs, exeors., admors. and assigns, and that free from the debts, controul or intermeddling of her husband. I hereby revoke all former wills by me at any time heretofore made and I appoint **Nicholas Murphy,** of Patrick's Hill, in the liberties of the City of Cork, Distiller; **Daniel Murphy,** the younger son of the said Daniel Murphy, hereinbefore named, and the said **Charles James Curtin,** executors of this, my will. In witness whereof, I have hereunto set my name and affixed my seal, this tenth day of October, one thousand eight hundred and thirty-five.

Elizabeth Lillis (Seal).

Signed, sealed, published and declared by the. Testatrix as and for her last Will and Testament in the presence of us who in her presence, at her request, and in the presence of each other have hereunto subscribed our names as witnesses thereto:

Jno. Bernard, M. D.,
William Magrath, Solr.,
Thomas Barry, Writing Clerk of the said Wm.
Magrath.

I certify that the foregoing is a true and authentic copy made pursuant to the Statute, 30 and 31 Vic., c. 70.

(Seal Public Record Office, Ireland)

Henry F. Berry
A. D. K.
13 February, 1902.

WILL.

PUBLIC RECORD OFFICE OF IRELAND.

Certified Copy of
A Record in the Public Record Office of Ireland,
Entitled:
Will of Richard Shine, 1777, Diocese of Cork and Ross.

In the name of God, amen, I, Richard Shine, of the Town of Passage, in the County of Cork, Victualler, being weak in body, but of sound and disposing mind and memory, thanks to almighty God for the same, do hereby make and publish this, my last Will and Testament, in manner and following hereby revoking all former and other wills or codicils by me heretofore made: First, I give, devise and bequeath unto my three dearly and well beloved grandchildren, to-wit: Joseph, Jonathan and Catherine, the sons and daughter of my son, John Shine, of Passage, aforesaid farmer, and the survivors and survivor of them and the executors, administrators, and assigns of such survivor, all my right, title and interest of, in and to that part of the Lands of Monks Town, in the said County of Cork, now in my possession, held by lease for a term of years yet to run and unexpired at and under the yearly rent or sum of seven pounds, eleven shillings and five pence, they or the survivors or survivor and the executors, administrators and assigns of such survivor duly paying thereout yearly and every year unto Mary White, daughter of Anthony White, formerly of or near Innishanon, in said County, deceased, the sum of twenty shillings ster. during the continuance of said lease, provided she shall so long live with Liberty for her the said Mary White and her assigns in case of not payment of said yearly annuity of twenty shillings ster. to enter said lands and distrain the same and dispose of said distress for said yearly annuity and the expense attending such distraining according to law, the first payment to be made in twelve months after my decease, and I, leave and bequeath my said two grandsons, Joseph and Jonathan, all my cows, horses, sheep, hay, corn and potatoes, which I shall die possessed of or entitled to be held in common between them or to be equally divided, share and share alike, and all my part of the Houses and Haggard on said Lands of Monkstown and all Implements of Husbandry thereunto belonging, together with the sum of eighty pounds ster. to my grandson, Joseph, and the like sum of Eighty pounds to my said other grandson, Jonathan. I also give, devise and bequeath unto my said granddaughter, Catherine Shine, her Executors, Administrators and Assigns, all my right, title and interest of, in and to that part of the lands of Pembrokestown, in said County, which was lately purchased by me from Charles Cotterell of Passage aforesaid, Publican, and now in the possession of William Pharisey, together with the sum of One hundred pounds ster. and one bed and bed clothes and a silver cup and brewing pan, and I do hereby order and direct that if the principal sum or any other part thereof, out of which said legacies are to accrue and be paid, shall not be at interest, at the time of my deceased, that the same shall be put to interest by and with the Joint Consent of my Executors and my said grandsons, and my will is that the aforesaid, several and respective legacies, together with their several and respective propositions of the interest money arising thereout be paid to my said grandchildren at their several and respective ages of twenty-one years and in case any of my beforementioned grandchildren shall happen to die before they arrive to the said age of twenty-one years, my will is that their proportion or proportions be and shall go to the survivors or survivor of them, and I order and direct that if my said son, John Shine, or any other person or persons shall commence any suit against any of my Executors on account of this, my will, that then the sum of Ten pounds shall be taken out of the legacy or legacies from each of my said grandchildren's share so as to make up a fund of Thirty pounds to support any suit the said John Shine or any other person or persons shall or may commence on account of this, my will. I also give and bequeath unto my granddaughter by marriage, Mary White Spinster, her choice of the beat bed and bed cloaths in my house, also six pewter plates, two pewter dishes, three silver table spoons, six silver tea spoons, one pair of brass chandlesticks and four chairs. I also give and bequeath unto my cousin, John Bradfield, for his honesty and service, the bed he now lies on, together with the bed cloaths of the same and one pair of brass candlesticks, and I will and desire that the remainder of my furniture not herein disposed of shall be equally and fairly divided between my said three grandchildren. I also give and bequeath unto my grandchildren, by marriage, Edward Ford, son of Michael Ford, of Passage, aforesaid, ship carpenter, and Margaret Ford, daughter of the said Michael, the sum of Five pounds each, to be paid them at their respective ages of Twenty-one years, and if either of them shall happen to dye before the age of twenty one years, then and in such case the survivor shall have the share of the other, and in case both should dye before they arrive to the age of Twenty-one years, then and in such case their respective proportions shall go to their father, the said Michael Ford. I also give and bequeath unto my son, John Shine, the sum of one hundred shillings, and no more, to be paid him if demanded immediately after my decease, he having heretofore received from me more than his proportion of my wordly substance and has turned out a disobedient son. I also desire and direct that all outstanding debts, which shall be due to me at the time of my decease, be applyed to discharge any debts I may owe to any person at the time aforesaid, and if there should any money remain after discharging my said debts, the same shall go to my said grandchildren's legacy, except there is as much as will defray said charges or any part of them at the time of my decease, in my possession, and if there shall be more than will defray said charges, the remainder shall go to be equally divided between my said three grandchildren, and lastly, I hereby nominate, constitute and appoint, John Dorman, of Rafeen, in the County of Cook, Esquire Michael Parker, of Passage, in said County, Esquire, and John Roberts, of Passage, aforesaid: Gentlemen executors of this my last will and testament, in witness whereof I have hereunto put my hand and seal, this thirty-first day of October, in the year of our Lord, One Thousand Seven Hundred and Seventy-five.

Richard Shine. (Seal.)

Signed, sealed, published and declared by the above named Richard Shine, to be his last will and testament in the presence of us, who have hereunto subscribed our names as witnesses in the presence of the Testator and in the presence of each other:

James Lawrence,
Michael Foord,
Robert Stransburg.

I, the within named Richard Shine, of Passage, aforesaid, do this Thirty-first day of October, One Thousand, Seven Hundred and Seventy-five, make and publish this as a Codicil, to my annexed Will and Testament, in manner following (that is to say), that in order to prevent any law suit, I hereby give and bequeath to my son, John Shine, of Passage, aforesaid, the sum of Two Hundred pounds ster., which I owe to my said son, John, the same to be paid him in a convenient and proper time after my decease. In witness whereof, I have hereunto put my hand and seal the day and year above written.

Signed, sealed, published and declared by the above named Richard Shine, as a Codicil to his annexed last will and testament in presence of us:

James Lawrence,
Michael Foord,
Robert Stransburg.

The 8th day of December, 1777, this will and codicil were Proved in common form of law and decreed valid and registered and administered with the will and codicil annexed, was granted and committed to Henry Hiers, in trust for the Legatees named in said will (John Dorman, Michael Parker and John Roberts, the executors therein named having renounced), being sworn and to return an Invey by 8th day of December next, in an account when required.

John Smith, Surgt.
Ths. Gregg, D. Regt.

I certify that the following is a true and authentic copy made pursuant to the Statute, 30 and 31 Vic., c. 70.

J. J. Digger La Gouche,
Deputy Keeper.
23 September, 1898.

WILL.

Certified Copy of
A Record in the Public Record Office of Ireland,
Entitled:
Will of Katherine Shine, 1732, Diocese of Cloyne.

In the name of God, amen, the fifteenth day of Febry., Seventeen hundred and twenty-one, I, Katherine Shine, of Macroone, in the County of Cork, being sick and weake in body, but of sound and perfect memory (praise be given to God for the same, do make this my last Will and Testament, hereby revoking, annulling and makeing void all wills, and testaments heretofore by me made and declared either by word or writeing.

Impr—I give and bequeath my soule to God, and my Body to be Bury'd after such manner as my Exrs. hereafter named shall think fitt.

Item—I give and bequeath unto my brother, John Geffors, the sum of five pounds sterl.

Item—I give and bequeath unto my granddaughter, Katherine Combs, the sum of twenty pounds sterl.

Item—I give and bequeath unto my grandson, Thomas Combs, the sum of ten pounds sterl.

Item—I give and bequeath unto my grandson, Michael Combs, the sum of ten pounds sterl.

Item—I give and bequeath unto my niece, Katherine Bowdle, the sum of one pound, ten shillings sterl.

Item—I give and bequeath unto my niece, Mary Cammigge, the sum of one pound ten shillings sterl.

Item—I give and bequeath unto my daughter, Frances Combs, all the rest of my worldly goods and substances, she paying all the debts I justly owe, and my funeral expenses.

Lastly—I appoint and nominate the Reverend William Jension and Robert Warren, Esqr., my sole executors, to see and have this, my Will and

Testament, duly executed. Wittness my hand and seal the day and year first above written.

Katherine X Shine. (Seal).
(Her mark and seal.)

Signed, sealed, published and declared by the above Katherine Shine, in the presence of us:

Natn. Haly,
William Liddy Junior,
Jam Morrogh.
(In dorso)

Probat fuit introscript Testum in Coi Juris Forma Vicesimo Octavo Die Mensis Aprilis As Dne 1732 coram Rendo Robt Bulfell Clero Vigore Comiois ad dict Effect ei direct emanat, Comissumg fuit & est Onus Execuois dti Testi una cum Admiaoe oium & Slor bonor &c introscript Catherine Shine deftoe Rendo Guliel Jennison Clico un ex Exccurious in testo Picto noiat juxta Tabutas tesar Primitus &c Jurat Roberto Warren ar alter Execure in eodem testo Constitut onus Execuois ejusd prius Renunciant Salvo Jure Cujuscung Dat 1 die May As Dne 1732

Jacobs Hanning Regruis.

I certify that the foregoing is a true and authentic copy made pursuant to the Statute 30 & 31 Vic., c. 70.

Sam Mills, D. N. A.
7 July, 1903.

WILL.

PUBLIC RECORD OFFICE OF IRELAND.

A Record in the Public Record Office of Ireland,
Entitled:
Will of Timothy Shine, 1777. (Diocess of Cork and Ross.)

In the name of God, amen: I, Timothy Shine, of Cooleen, parish of Inshegeelae, County Cork, being weak in body, but sound in mind and memory and knowing the uncertainty of this freal life, do make this, my last Will and Teatament, revoking and annulling all and every Will or Wills, hereto fore made by me, to-wit: imprimis—I bequeath my soul to the mercy of my worthy savour, Jesus Christ, humbly creaving and expecting his mercy through the merits of his bitter passion, as to my wordly substance, I leave it in manner following:

I bequeath unto my son, Dinis Shine, Five shillings, together with my best suit of cloaths or wearing apperel. I bequeath unto my son, Daniel Shine, five shillings, and unto my son, Timothy Shine, Five shillings, unto my daughter, Mary Croneen, alias Shine, Five shillings, unto my daughter, Julian Keleher, alias Shine, Five shillings. The remainder of my wordly substance, real and personal, I leave and bequeath unto my dearly beloved wife, Julian Shine, alias Sullivan. I appoint and constitute Denis O'Leary, Esq., of Will Street, Tim O'Leary of Glasheen, and my dearly beloved wife, Julian Shine, to be ye exequetors of this, my last Will and Testiment, in witness whereof, I subscribe my hand and seal this Twenty-seventh day of January, One thousand, seven hundred and seventy-seven (1777).

Tim Shine (Seal).

Signed, sealed and published in presence of:

Daniel Nevil,
John Cronin.

The 4th July, 1777, this Will was performed in common form of law and decreed valid and registered and the burthen of the exn thereof and administered of the goods and of the deceased where granted and committed

116

to Julian Shine, one of the Exrs. named (saving the right of the other Exrs.); she being sworn and to return an Invty by 4th January next and an account when required.

John Smith, Surgt.
Thos. Gregg, D. Rr.

I certify that the foregoing is a true and authentic copy made pursuant to the Statute, 30 & 31 Vic., c. 70.

John Overendoverend,
The Assistant Deputy Keeper of the Record.
22nd Sept., 1898.

www.ingramcontent.com/pod-product-compliance
Lightning Source LLC
Chambersburg PA
CBHW030255030426
42336CB00009B/387